I Talk with God:
The Art of Prayer and Meditation for Catholic Children

Compiled and Edited by
Janet P. McKenzie, OCDS

Biblio Resource Publications
108½ South Moore Street
Bessemer, MI 49911
2011

©2011 by Janet P. McKenzie

All right reserved. No part of this book may be reproduced, stored in a retrieval system, or transmitted, in any form or by any means, electronic, mechanical, photocopying, recording, or otherwise, without the written permission of the copyright holder.

ISBN 978-1-934185-40-7

Published by Biblio Resource Publications, Inc.
108½ South Moore Street, Bessemer, MI 49911
info@biblioresource.com

A **R**ead **A**loud **C**urriculum **E**nrichment Product
www.RACEforHeaven.com

The Children of the Lantern by "Lamplighter"
Nihil Obstat: Carolus Davis, S.T.L., *Censor Deputatus*
Imprimatur: Georgius L. Cravin, *Episcopus Sebastopolos*, 1958

The Little Children's Prayer Book by Mother Mary Loyola
Imprimatur: Josephus Robertus, 1911

Jesus Bless Me by Sister M. Imelda, S.L
Nihil Obstat: John M. Fearns, S.T.D., *Censor Librorum*
Imprimatur: Francis Cardinal Spellman, *Archbishop of New York*, 1955

A Week of Communions by "Lamplighter"
Nihil Obstat: Innocentius Apap, S.TH.M., O.P., *Censor Deputatus*
Imprimatur: Joseph Butt, Vicar General, 1936

Scripture texts in this work are taken from the *New American Bible with Revised New Testament* © 1986, 1970 Confraternity of Christian Doctrine, Washington, D.C. and are used by permission of the copyright owner. All Rights Reserved. No part of the *New American Bible* may be reproduced in any form without permission in writing from the copyright owner.

Printed in the United States of America

Contents

Talking with God .... i-ii

Section I: Different Ways of Talking with God—
   A Read-Aloud Selection 1-14

Section II: Many Ways to Pray 15-73
   I Pray Every Day 17-21
      Morning Prayers 17-18
      My Daytime Prayers 18-20
      My Night Prayers 20-21
   I Pray the Mass 22-35
   I Pray the Sacraments 36-45
      Confession 36-40
      Communion Prayers 40-43
      We Renew Baptismal Vows 43-45
   I Pray My Devotions 46-64
      The Way of the Cross 46-50
      Benediction 50-51
      The Rosary 51-56
      The Scapular 57
      The Miraculous Medal 57-58
      I Visit Our Lord 58-60
      I Visit My Angel 60-61
      I Visit Our Lady 61-63
      I Visit St. Joseph 63-64
   I Obey 65-66
      The Commandments of the Church 65
      The Commandments of God 65-66
   I Live in the World 67-68

I Love God 69-73
   Walking with Our Father 69-70
   Working for Our Father 71-73

Section III: Meditation 75-113
   To the Boys and Girls Who Use These
      Meditations 77-79
   Jesus Teaches Me How to Talk
      with God 81-96
   I Talk with God in Holy Communion ... 97-98
   The Gospels Teach Me How to
      Talk with God 99-103
   Talk with God in Meditation 105-110
   I Talk with God through the Prayer of
      St. Thomas Aquinas 111-113

Section IV: Prayer and Meditation 115-122
   Find a Holy Place 117
   Keep a Holy Quiet 117-118
   Stay in Holy Stillness 118
   Talk with Loving Words 118-119
   Listen to God 119-120
   Read-aloud Children's Books on Prayer
      and Meditation 121
   Adult Resources on Children's Prayer 122

More RACE for Heaven Products 123-131

Talking with God

What is prayer? Sometimes prayer seems mysterious and hard to understand. Sometimes it is hard to pray. Sometimes you may worry that you do not know how to talk with God. You may not know what to say to Him.

St. Teresa of Avila, who died in 1582, wrote several books about prayer. She said that prayer is nothing more than a friendly conversation with our loving God. St. Teresa tells us that, in prayer, it is important not to talk much or to think much but only to love much. In prayer, what we say to God is not as important as just loving Him.

According to St. Teresa, you do not need to go out looking for God to tell Him that you love Him, for if you are in the state of grace, He lives right inside you. In order to pray, you need only to find a place to be alone with God. In silence, you can pray by loving the God who dwells within your heart.

The purpose of this book is not to teach you how to pray—that is between you and God—but to explain what prayer and meditation are and to show you how easy they are to do.

This book gives examples of the many forms that prayer can take. It contains prayers to pray out loud (vocal prayer) or to pray in the silence of your heart. It shows how you can talk with God, and, more importantly, how you can love God. It talks about using pictures and images—like holy cards and the Stations of the Cross—to help you pray and meditate. This book also shows you how to use Bible stories to learn the lessons Jesus taught. You will see how you can pray to God silently in the quiet of your room, in church, or outdoors in His wonderful creation—any where, any place.

As you progress through this book—from discovering what prayer is to reciting simple prayers to understanding meditation and then to helps for moving into deeper meditation—you will see that prayer and meditation often go together. Meditation is described by the big *Catechism of the Catholic Church* as "prayerful reflection." So meditation is really nothing more than *holy thinking*. You can use books, devotions, pictures, holy cards, and images (such as stained glass windows in church) to help you think or meditate on holy people, events, and ideas.

I hope this book will help you become more comfortable about talking with God. My prayer for you is that each day you take time to talk with God so you can love God more and become closer friends. I pray that you learn to hear His voice and follow His holy will so that everything you think, do and say will be pleasing to Him.

Janet P. McKenzie
Feast of the Triumph of the Cross
September 14, 2011

"Different Ways of
Talking with God"

A Read-Aloud Selection
from
The Children of the Lantern

by
"Lamplighter"

The following story is Chapter 9 from the book, *The Children of the Lantern* (1958). In this book, a nun in Rome (the "Lamplighter") who teaches Saturday "lantern lessons," to children, aged four to eleven—taking them through the catechism step-by-step using pictures, stories, and real life experiences.

Different Ways of Talking with God

"I like thinking about God, and talking to Him," said Elizabeth one day, "but I don't like saying my prayers!"

It was this comment of Elizabeth's that made the Lamplighter decide that we must have one whole lesson on prayer because, of course, Elizabeth would not *dislike* saying her prayers if she had properly understood that they *were* just what she said she *liked,* "thinking about God, and talking to Him."

Perhaps there are other children who think of "saying prayers" as one thing, and "talking to God" as something different, and if so—as that is the very greatest pity—this lesson will, it is hoped, show them that they are making a big mistake, and help them to see that prayer rightly understood is a very easy, and a very lovely, happy thing.

After we had sung our hymn to the Holy Child, there appeared on the screen a card with these words:

Different Ways of Praying

1. Just thinking
2. Just looking
3. Thanking
4. Being sorry
5. Being glad
6. Making up
7. Slow words
8. Giving
9. Asking

They were written in different colors, and the Lamplighter said, "We'll take those different ways in turn, and I expect those of you who have been coming for some time to the lantern lessons to help me to give this one. Some of you know quite a lot about talking to God, but others, who have only begun to come lately, are, I think, in a little bit of a muddle about prayer, thinking of it as just something that must be *done,* not enjoyed!

"As we are going to begin with the prayer of 'just thinking', here is a picture of a friend of mine for you to look at first.

🙌 "'Prayer is the lifting up of the mind and heart to God,' the catechism[1] says. To raise, or lift up, your minds to God is then only another way of saying *'thinking of God',* and that in itself is praying."

---
[1] See Question 475 of the revised *Baltimore Catechism* of 1941.

Different Ways of Talking with God

"But is that little girl praying?" asked Jane.

"I don't know. She is certainly *thinking*."

"Yes, she's having a good 'think'," said Renata.

"She hadn't the least idea she was being photographed," said the Lamplighter. "Someone saw her sitting in a lovely garden, all by herself, near a lilac bush—having a good 'think' as you say—and took the photo.

"Perhaps she *is* thinking of God and saying 'Thank you for this lovely garden to sit in'.

"That would be a very good prayer, wouldn't it, and though it belongs really to 'thanking prayers', she thanked only because she had first been *thinking*."

"I've tried the thinking-of-God prayers a lot," said Magda, "because in our church it's so dark that I can't always use my missal-book, and sometimes there are such big fat people in the bench in front of me that I can't even see the altar!"

"Well, if Magda makes the best of the dark and the crowd, and just turns her thoughts to God, isn't she making a good prayer?"

"Yes!" and Silvia added, "Of course, you'd have different thoughts, if it was Mass, to your Benediction-thoughts and—"

"And different ones too," broke in Pietro, "if Mommy just took you in to church for a minute to visit with *Il Santissimo*."

("The Most Holy"—that is the beautiful name for our Lord in the tabernacle, which you hear in Rome.)

"But there's no *time* to think at your morning and night prayers," said Giovannino. "Miss always says to me: 'Nino, be quick and say your prayers!'"

I Talk with God

(Italian children always call their English governess "Miss" as English children call their French one *"Mademoiselle."*)

The children laughed at Giovannino's funny voice, but someone said, "That's just what Mommy says to me: 'Hurry up and say your prayers!'"

"I'm quite sure that the 'Quick' when 'Miss' or your mother says it, isn't meant for *the prayers*," said the Lamplighter, "but for *stopping doing something else*, when it's time for prayers!"

"Yes. P'raps," said someone.

— stopping doing something else when its time for prayers —

"Now you all see, don't you, that we can pray very well by just turning those thoughts of ours which are always on *something*, to God, to our Lord, to Jesus as a child—as a tiny baby, or as a boy, or as a man suffering for us, and asking Him to keep those flighty minds of ours fixed on the thought of Him for a little while. It is not difficult really, and by degrees we get better at it, as we do at anything we do often, and then, gradually, we get into a *habit* of thinking of God, and it has become quite easy!

"'*Just looking*.' That way of praying you all know, and of course it turns into 'just thinking'. You all love pictures, don't you?"

A tremendously loud "yes" came from all the lantern children.

"You love *some* pictures better than others, of course, and not all of you like the same, but, at the lantern lessons you have plenty of choice, and some of you have told me that you 'take them away in your head' and can see them again quite easily."

"I can!"

"And so can I!"

"Well, that's a great help in our prayers. We 'just look' at our Lady, with the Baby in her arms, or at the Holy Child teaching the doctors in the Temple, or at our Lord with the children around Him, or walking on the Sea of Galilee, or carrying His Cross, and at once we are in touch with Him, near Him, learning something from Him, without perhaps quite knowing that we are, and it's as easy as possible to talk to Him in just any way we like. . . .

"The great Pope St. Gregory, who lived in the sixth century, thought that pictures could help us very much. It was he who said, 'In a picture, he who has no letters may yet read.'

"So let us ask our Lord to paint lots of pictures of Him and His mother and the saints on our minds, and on our hearts, during our lessons, so that we may carry them home and turn them into prayers, whenever we like.

"Now about the prayer of *'thanking:'*

"How do we know that our Lord likes to be thanked?"

"Because everyone does!"

"Well, they do, I think, and our Lord, being 'truly man'—really like us that is—must be the same, but that we may be quite *sure* that He is, there is a story in His life. . . ."

"I know!" said Jill. "The one about those ten men He cured, and when only one came back to say 'thank you', our Lord asked where the others were[2], and in the picture you showed us, He looked very sad."

"That's right, there it is, to look at again. We must not be among the ungrateful 'nine'— we have so many, many nice things to thank God for, and new ones every day, but it *is* strange that we say fewer 'thanking' prayers than perhaps any others—certainly fewer than 'asking' ones. We say:

"'Please God, let it be fine tomorrow!'

"'Please send me a bicycle at Christmas!'

"'Please let me pass my exam!'

"And when it *is* fine, and we get our bicycle, and do *well* in our exam, we are so delighted that we forget all about thanking."

"Well, don't let's!" said Niccolo.

"No, don't let's!" said the Lamplighter.

"The *being sorry* prayer comes next."

"That's saying our act of contrition," said Magda, "telling God we're sorry for our sins—we say it at our night prayers, and when we go to confession."

"That's quite true, but I was thinking of the *'being*

---

[2] See St. Luke 17:15-19.

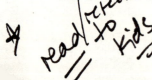

Different Ways of Talking with God

sorry'—not so much of the words in which we say it. We learn an act of contrition—or sorrow—by heart, of course, but do the actual *words* matter to our Lord?"

"No," Renata replied, "not if we are sorry. We can say it in any words."

"That is what I want you all to remember. Once in England, I was preparing a little boy for his first confession, and one day he said: 'But what should I do if *I forget* my act of contrition, if the words go out of my head?' He was troubled about it at first, but he was quite happy when he understood that it did not matter if he forgot the words he had learnt by heart—that our Lord understands all about forgetting, and that if he said over and over again, while the priest gave him absolution: 'I'm sorry—I'm sorry—You love me—You died for me—for my sins—please forgive me. I will try to be good. Please help me to be very sorry, and not to do these sins again' . . . and *meant* those words, he had made a very good act of contrition.

"Our just looking' prayer helps us with our 'being sorry'. We look at one of those pictures we have collected in our minds—our Lord in the Garden, or being crowned with thorns, or nailed to the Cross, and then we THINK about it. Remember, too, that our making up our minds to try to be better—what the Catechism calls 'a *firm purpose of amendment'*—is the test of whether we are really sorry, not the *feeling* sorry. It isn't a question so much of our feelings as of our *wills,* helped, of course, by God, who will never refuse that help—the help to overcome our faults.

"We'll leave the *being glad* prayer for a moment, because the *making-up* one fits best on to *being sorry.*"

"You mean when we do small good things to make up for being bad, don't you?" said Silvia, "like the prayers the priest gives us to say when we go to confession."

"Yes, of course, those prayers 'make up'—or 'make satisfaction for our sins' as the Catechism puts it—more than any others we could say for ourselves, just because they are part of the sacrament—but I was thinking of other things, too, we might do to make up when we haven't been good.

"One of the best is taking cheerfully—*for that reason*—our small sufferings, our disappointments, our lessons, when we're not inclined to study—all those can be turned into very good prayers of making-up.

"*Being glad* is a nice happy kind of prayer, and it suits some times better than others. Which of you Bigger People can explain what I mean?"

"I know," said Jill. "Easter's one good time for it—being glad our Lord's sufferings are over, and that He has risen out of the tomb!"

"And Christmas! It's easy to be glad then," said John.

"Yes, but glad not only for the plum pudding (though perhaps that's too English a dish for you Romans) and the Christmas tree and the presents, but glad for *God's* side of it. Glad that each Christmas keeps in memory the day He became Man, and was born a little child, to live on earth with us, and atone for our sins, and to give the gift of divine life which we all receive through Baptism. It is that life which is our *real* life, the one which is going to last always in heaven, so it's something to be very glad indeed about.

"Now do always remember the morning offering of which we've spoken so often. The little rhymed one if you like. Or, here is another: 'My God, I offer You the prayers, work, joys, and sufferings of this day, for all the intentions of Your divine heart in the Holy Mass.'

"That is the prayer *of giving,* which is the eighth kind of prayer on our list. You give our Lord *everything* in that prayer, and even things not a bit holy in themselves, like our meals, and our games, may *become* holy in that way, as we've often said before, but can't say *too* often because it's so important.

"Again the *words* don't matter! Make up morning offerings for yourselves: 'Today I want to do everything to please You. I love You, Jesus, and I want to give You all I can, so I give You all my day.'

"You all know how to say things like that to God, and He does *really* love to hear them."

"Is the morning offering enough prayers to say when we get up?" asked Jane.

"Quite enough if we say this with all our heart, really meaning what we say—and much better than a lot of prayers said badly, and inattentively, and without a bit of love in them, but it is nice to add the Our Father, and the Hail Mary and—when we are older—the Creed, and the short Acts of Faith, Hope and Love, and, of course, all our 'God bless' prayers: Mommy and Daddy and the others. But what I want you all to see is that it is the prayers being *real* and *loving,* not their number, that pleases God.

"All that applies to our night prayers as well, and it is a good thing at the end to stop for a few minutes, and think how we have behaved ourselves during the day; if we have done anything that has displeased God, and then—if we remember things like that—to be sorry about them, and tell God so, and ask Him to help us to be better tomorrow.

"I put the *prayer of asking* on our list, but I don't think you need to be told much about that! We all know how to ask for what we want—the thing is to try, as we get older and have more sense, to want the things that will make us more pleasing to God, more like Him, more able to work for Him—things for our souls, that is—the part of us that really matters—as well as things for our bodies, for, of course, we may ask for those too.

"Now to end, I want to tell you why I put *the prayer of slow words* on our list of ways of talking with God.

"I was once preparing a boy for his first confession. His name was Noel (that is, as some of you know, French for 'Christmas,' and they called him that because he was born on Christmas Eve), and he was seven. The first day he came for a lesson (I suppose because he wanted to show me all that he knew), he said, 'Listen how fast I can say the Our Father!' and then he rattled it off from beginning to end, and seemed quite proud of himself.

"Poor Noel! He was a very nice little man, and sensible, and he soon saw that that was not a prayer at all, when he understood—as I hope you all do now—what prayer really is.

"Look at the screen now, and you will see the Our Father, the *Pater Noster*—as some call it—written out as what we may call a 'prayer of slow words.' The Italic print is for our *thoughts*."

OUR FATHER . . . *This is the best prayer I can say to You, God, because You made it Yourself.*

WHO ART IN HEAVEN . . . *Please let me be in heaven some day, and everyone else too—all of us who are Your children, because we're baptized.*

HALLOWED BE THY NAME . . . *Your Name is holy. Make more and more people know Your Name and love it, and You, and try to serve You. Please let me too.*

THY KINGDOM COME . . . *That means "Don't only be King of heaven, but of our hearts." If You are our King now, You will be sure to take us to Your kingdom in heaven.*

THY WILL BE DONE . . . *I often want my own way—my own will—and sometimes it isn't Your way, Your will.*

ON EARTH AS IT IS IN HEAVEN . . . *When it isn't, don't let me have it. Help us all to do what You want—like people in heaven do.*

GIVE US THIS DAY OUR DAILY BREAD . . . *Please give us every day the things we need. Things like our food, for our bodies, but more still the things that help our souls—especially Holy Communion. You would like us to receive You every day. I will try my best to go to Holy Communion as often as I can.*

I Talk with God

FORGIVE US OUR TRESPASSES AS WE . . . *If we want You to forgive us our sins, and all the things You don't like us to do (and we do want You to, please God), then I know we must be kind and forgiving, instead of being angry with people who do things we don't like.*

FORGIVE THOSE WHO TRESPASS AGAINST US . . . *We want You to forgive us and so we must forgive those who annoy us and anger us.*

AND LEAD US NOT INTO TEMPTATION . . . *Temptation means feeling we'd like to do wrong things—Help us not to listen, not to give in!*

BUT DELIVER US FROM EVIL . . . *Keep all bad things away from us.*

AMEN . . . *"Amen" means—please do all we've asked in this prayer!*

"There was a very holy woman called Margery Kempe, who lived in England, many hundreds of years ago now, but whose name is remembered, because of her great love of our Lord, and of her "talking" with Him.

"She has left us some writings in which she says very interesting things about prayer. Here is just *one* —about the thing of which we have been speaking— that it isn't a *lot of words* that make prayer, and that *loving thoughts* of God are far better than just words that we don't understand, and so cannot be called talking to God at all.

"You Bigger People will know now what Margery Kempe means, 'You shall have more merit in heaven for ONE YEAR THINKING IN YOUR MIND than for A HUNDRED YEARS OF PRAYING WITH YOUR MOUTH.'"

Many Ways to Pray

Prayers from Two Children's Prayer Books:

Jesus Bless Me
By Sister M. Imelda

and

The Little Children's Prayer Book
By Mother Mary Loyola

I Pray Every Day

My Morning Prayers

(handwritten margin note: do as exercise if kids)

I make the Sign of the Cross saying, "In the name of the Father and of the Son and of the Holy Spirit. Amen."

I think. I keep still.
God gave me this new day because He loves me. What good thing will I do today to show God how much I love Him?

"O my God, because I love You, I am going to . . . Please, help me do it.
Blessed Mother, help me to be good today. Amen."

My Morning Offering

"O my God, I offer You every thought and word and action of today. Please, bless me, O God, and make me good today. Amen."

My Morning Offering Poem

"My God, I offer You this day,
All I think or do or say.
Uniting it with what was done
On earth by Jesus Christ, Your Son. Amen."

Hail Mary

"Hail Mary, full of grace! The Lord is with thee. Blessed art thou among women, and blessed is the fruit of thy womb, Jesus. Holy Mary, Mother of God, pray for us sinners, now, and at the hour of our death. Amen."

Our Father

"Our Father, who art in heaven, hallowed be Thy name. Thy kingdom come. Thy will be done on earth as it is in heaven. Give us this day our daily bread; and forgive us our trespasses, as we forgive those who trespass against us; and lead us not into temptation, but deliver us from evil. Amen."

"Mother of Mercy, pray for us."

My Guardian Angel

"Angel of God, my guardian dear, to whom God's love commits me here. Ever this day be at my side, to light and guard, to rule and guide. Amen."

Glory Be

"Glory be to the Father and to the Son and to the Holy Spirit. As it was in the beginning, is now, and ever shall be, world without end. Amen."

My Daytime Prayers

"Dear Jesus, I promised You to try to be good. Do help me all this day to try my best. Mother Mary, help me. Amen."

1. Love God

I must go to Mass on Sunday if I can.
It will please You very much if I go every day.
I must try to pray well.
Every prayer I say I must say well.
I will not pray in a hurry.

Many Ways to Pray

2. Love My Neighbor
I must obey my father and my mother, and all who are over me.

What I Must Do
I must be kind.
I must be helpful.
I must be honest.
I must tell the truth.

"Dear Jesus, if I try to do these things today, You will bless me today. If I try to do these things every day, I know I will be Your friend. Amen."

An Act of Faith
"O my God, I believe all the truths that the Holy Catholic Church teaches because You have told us so, and Your word is true. Amen."

An Act of Hope
"O my God, because You are all-powerful, merciful, and keep Your promises, I hope to be happy with You in heaven. Amen."

An Act of Love
"O my God, because You are all-good, I love You with my whole heart and soul. Amen."

"My Jesus, mercy!"

"Jesus, Mary, and Joseph, bless us now and at the hour of our death. Amen."

I Talk with God

BEFORE MEALS
Make the Sign of the Cross and say, "Bless us, O Lord, and these Thy gifts which we are about to receive from Thy bounty through Christ Our Lord. Amen."

AFTER MEALS
Make the Sign of the Cross and say, "We give You thanks, O Almighty God, who lives and reigns forever. May the souls of the faithful departed, through the mercy of God, rest in peace. Amen."

MY NIGHT PRAYERS
I make the Sign of the Cross and pray, "My God, I believe that You are here, that You see me, and hear me, and love me. I thank You for taking care of me today. Help me to see what sins I have done and to be sorry for them. Amen."

Then, I keep still for a while and think.
God gave me this day because He loves me.
What did I do with it?
Did I do anything to show God that I love Him?
If I did, Jesus is glad.
He will give me a heavenly gift for it.
I promised Jesus to do something. Did I do it?
I promised Jesus to try to be good today. Did I try?
Did I forget to try?

ON SUNDAY NIGHT
I must go to Mass on Sunday, if I can. Did I go?
What did I do? Did I try to pray?
A prayer book (or missal) helps me to pray well. Did I use my prayer book?

WEEK-DAY NIGHTS
It is a good thing to go to Mass.
It pleases Jesus.
Did I go?
Did I try to pray well?
Did I let my mind wander?
Was I good today?
Did I obey my father? Did I obey my mother? Did I obey my teacher?
Was I kind?
Was I helpful?
Was I modest?
Was I honest?
Did I tell the truth?

AN ACT OF CONTRITION
"O my God, I am sorry for all my sins because they displease You who are all-good and deserving of all my love. With Your help, I will sin no more. Amen."

Pray one Our Father, one Hail Mary, and the Sign of the Cross.

I Pray the Mass

THE SACRIFICE OF THE MASS

I am going to Mass, and I must think what this means. Mass is not only something *said*, it is something *done*. It is the holiest thing that can be done on earth. It is a Sacrifice. A sacrifice is something offered to God to show that he is the Master of all things. Because God is so great, so holy, and so good, we have to adore or worship Him. Because He has given us all we have, we must thank Him. Because we have offended this great and holy God, we must be sorry. And because we want many things for our souls and our bodies, we must ask Him for them.

Now, we cannot do any of these things properly by ourselves. We cannot adore Him enough, nor thank Him enough, nor be sorry enough for our sins, nor ask Him as we should for what we want. We are only poor tiny little creatures in God's sight. All this big world, and all the big worlds we see shining over our heads at night, are like specks of dust to Him—He is so great. We have nothing good enough to give Him. Thousands of gentle lambs and doves have been offered to God in sacrifice—but it was not enough. Not all the angels and saints, not our Blessed Lady herself, can give Him enough praise and love. Only our Lord Jesus Christ, who is God Himself, can give to God all He ought to have.

And so Jesus offered Himself as a sacrifice to His Father when He hung upon the Cross. *This was enough*. The sacrifice of Calvary paid to God all we owe Him, and bought us heaven and all we want to get there. But we have to bring into our souls the good things our Lord got for us on the Cross. There is plenty of water in the river, but unless we bring it into our houses, it is no good to us. How are we to get into our souls all our dear Lord died to give us? By the holy Mass.

The Mass is the same Sacrifice as that of Calvary. Our Lord is as truly on the altar as He was on the Cross. Only He does not die now. And we do not see Him offering His Sacrifice. He offers Himself by the hands of His priests. His Apostles were His first priests. At the Last Supper, they saw Him take bread into His holy hands and lift His eyes to heaven. They heard Him say over the bread, "This is My Body," and over the wine in the cup, "This is My Blood." Then He said, "Do this in memory of Me." What had He done? He had said the first Mass. He had consecrated, which means He had made holy, the bread and the wine by changing them into His holy Body and Blood. And He gave them power to do what He had done—to change bread into His Body, and wine into His Blood, and to pass on this power to the priests of His Church till He shall come again.

This is what is done at Mass. This is why the Mass is so great. One Mass pleases God more than all the songs of praise they sing in heaven. By one Mass we can thank Him as much as He deserves for all He has given us. And we can get from Him all that is good for us to have. I must try, then, always to go to Mass as I should.

I Talk with God

The Mass is the most perfect prayer because in it we adore, honor and glorify God, we thank Him for all His gifts, we ask Him to forgive us and we beg His graces and blessings.

My Prayers before Mass
(Kneel)
I am going to try my best to pray the Mass. I want to begin right. I will be on time. I will genuflect. I will go to my place. I will kneel and pray. Then I will sit down. I will be quiet. If I have to wait for Mass to begin, I will read my prayer book or missal.

The Beginning of Mass
Mass begins. I kneel. I begin to pray the Mass with the priest. The priest makes the Sign of the Cross. I make the Sign of the Cross with the priest. "In the name of the Father and of the Son and of the Holy Spirit. Amen."

O my God, I want to share in Your joy.
I want to receive Your blessings.

We Ask Forgiveness
I have sinned often.
I will ask for God's forgiveness.
I confess to God, to the Blessed Virgin, to the angels, to the saints, and to you, Father, that I have sinned. My sins are my fault, my own fault, my very own fault. I ask the Blessed Virgin, I ask all those who are in heaven, to pray for me.

"When I think, O dearest Jesus,
    What my sins have done to Thee.
How they in the lonely Garden
    Made Thee sad as sad could be.
I am very, very sorry
    To have given Thee such pain.
Do forgive, and bless, and help me
    That I may not sin again.
                        Amen."

WE SAY THE ANGELS' WORDS
This part of the Mass honors the birth of Jesus. We say the words the angels sang, "Glory to God!"

We praise You, God. We bless You. We adore You. We give You thanks.

"Before You came into this world, dear Lord, everyone was afraid of You. They knew You are the great God who made the world and the starry skies. They knew that You are All-Holy and that You hate sin. They knew that You can do all things and that the strongest man is less than a little fly in Your sight. And so they thought men would be afraid of You when You came upon the earth. They did not know that You would cry when You were cold and hungry, that when neighbors came into the cottage of Nazareth to see Mary's beautiful little baby, and took You into their arms, and smiled at You, You would smile back; that You would go out and play with other children, and come in when Your mother called, and fold Your little hands in prayer, before she put You to sleep. They did not know all this, or they would not have been afraid of You. How glad I am that I know it, that I did not live before You came, but now. You want me to love You, O little Child, and not to be afraid, now that You are coming so close to me, even into my heart. Dear little Jesus, I love You, I love You, come and let us love one another."

"My God, I am glad that by this Mass, You will be praised and loved as much as You deserve, because Jesus will love and praise You, and He is God. I want to do what He does, and to give You glory with Him. Glory be to the Father, and to the Son, and to the Holy Spirit. As it was in the beginning, is now and ever shall be, world without end. Amen."

We Read an Apostle's Letter
We now read a letter from a friend of Jesus to get us ready to read the words of Jesus. We thank God that we are Catholic.

We Read the Gospel
We stand to hear the words of Jesus Christ Himself, and make the Sign of the Cross on our forehead to show that we believe what Jesus Christ has taught us, on our lips to show we will never speak against it, and on our heart to show we love it and will do what He tells us.

Jesus often spoke to the people. He told them how to be good. The words He said are told in the Gospel. Now, we read some of the words of Jesus. Long ago, some boys and girls came to Jesus. They wanted Him to bless them. The Apostles stopped them, saying, "Go away!"

But Jesus said, "Let the children come to me. I want them." And Jesus blessed them.

Jesus, You are present here
    Just as tender, kind and dear
As in Jewish days of old
    When the little children bold
Climbed Your knee, and on Your breasts
    Laid their heads in happy rest.
I, a little one, may dare
    More than this, for I may share
Mary's joy, and now at last
    In my arms may hold You fast,
Have You for my very own,
    As if You were mine alone.
Oh how happy I must be
    When You come, Lord, to me!

A Gospel Meditation

There were two sisters who lived at Bethany. They were the friends of Jesus and were always looking forward to His visits and seeing what they could do to make Him welcome. Martha spared no trouble in getting ready for Him. She made the house clean and tidy and bright with flowers, and got out all her best things to show Him honor.

"Help me, dear Lord, to be like Martha when I am getting ready to receive You. Preparation for Holy Communion does not only mean saying some prayers just before. It means trying to please You in all I do, trying to remember that You see me when I kneel down to say my morning prayers, when I examine my conscience at night, when I go to Mass, and make my Act of Contrition before Confession. If I do these things as well as I can, and put away other thoughts when they come in prayer; if I learn my lessons well, and do as I am told because I want to please You, and take care not to say or do what would make You sad, then I am preparing for Holy Communion all day long. I am getting my little house ready for You like Martha. I am putting bright flowers about everywhere. And when You come, You will be quite pleased and love me more than You did before, and want to come again."

Because our Lord was pleased with Martha, He told her what He wanted her to do. I will sometimes hear Him speaking to my heart, and I will listen to Him and do what He tells me."

I Believe In God
(Stand)

I have read the words of Jesus. Now I tell Him that I believe in Him.
I believe in God, the Father Almighty.
I believe in Jesus.
He is God the Son.
He became Man.
His Mother is Mary.
He died on the cross.
He rose from the dead.
He went up to heaven.
He will come to judge us.
I believe in the Holy Spirit, the Catholic Church, and life in heaven.

Many Ways to Pray

WE OFFER BREAD AND WINE
(Sit)
The priest is ready to offer gifts to God. These gifts are bread and wine. Now, the bread is only bread. Soon it will be the Body of Jesus. Now, the wine is only wine. Soon it will be His Precious Blood.

Soon Jesus will offer Himself to God for me. He will be the Holy Gift offered to God. I give myself, too. I give myself to God.

"My God, You deserve more love and praise than all the men and women, and children in the world can give You. But Your Divine Son is coming down upon the altar to help us. He will adore You for us. He will thank You for all You have done for us. He will get us forgiveness of our sins and all the graces and blessings we need."

"Dear Lord, I thank You for all You are going to do for us. You are going to change the bread and wine into your holy Body and Blood. Change me too, Jesus, meek and humble heart; make my heart like unto Yours."

Ah! What gift or present,
    Jesus, can I bring?
I have nothing worthy
    Of my God and King.
But You are my Shepherd,
    I, Your little lamb;
Take *myself*, dear Jesus,
    All I have and am.
Take my body, Jesus,
    Eyes, and ears, and tongue

Never let them, Jesus,
    Help to do You wrong.
Take my heart, and fill it
    Full of love for Thee.
All I have I give Thee,
    Give Yourself to me.

THE PRIEST WASHES HIS HANDS

The priest washes his hands. He prepares for the Sacrifice. We ask God to make our souls clean. We want to offer the Holy Sacrifice.

"Dear Jesus, I too am to touch You today. You will rest upon my tongue. Your Sacred Heart will be close to mine. Oh, how holy I ought to be! Give me a clean heart. Wash away all my sins and take care of me that I may not sin again.

WE PRAY TO GOD

The bell rings to tell us that Jesus is coming.
(Kneel)
Now the holiest part of the Mass begins. Soon the bread and wine will become Jesus. I kneel and pray, "Holy, Holy, Holy: Lord God of the angels! Heaven and earth are full of Your glory."

Jesus will offer Himself to God. He will offer Himself to God for me.

"Blessed Mother, help me to offer myself to God.

WE HONOR GOD

The priest asks God to bless us. Jesus asked His Father to give Him courage to suffer.

On the cross, Jesus offered Himself to God. Jesus was the priest and the gift. In the Mass, Jesus acts through the priest at the altar. Jesus again truly offers Himself to God.

Jesus again is truly the priest. He is the gift. Jesus acts through the priest at the altar. In a moment, Jesus will be on the altar.

Jesus Comes

Jesus took bread. He gave thanks. He blessed the bread. He gave it to His Apostles, "Take and eat; for this is My Body."

The priest now uses the power of Jesus to change the bread into His living Body. The priest does what Jesus did.

Now Jesus is here. The priest raises the Host for us to adore the living Body of Jesus. I look at the Host. It is Jesus.

I say, "My Lord and my God."

Jesus Is Here

Jesus took the cup of wine. He gave thanks to God. He blessed the wine. Jesus gave the wine to His Apostles, "Drink this, for this is My Blood."

The priest does what Jesus did. He prays over the wine. He changes the wine into the living Blood of Jesus.

Now Jesus is here. The priest raises the cup containing the Precious Blood which Jesus shed for us.

I look at it. I say, "My Jesus, mercy.

We Pray for the Dead
O God, we offer You a pure Gift and a holy Gift. We ask You to be merciful to the Holy Souls.

We ask You to bless all of us poor sinners for whom Your Son Jesus was born, died on the Cross, rose from the dead, and went up to heaven to prepare the way for us.

We Pray the Our Father
"Our Father, who art in heaven, hallowed be Thy name. Thy kingdom come. Thy will be done on earth as it is in heaven. Give us this day our daily bread; and forgive us our trespasses as we forgive those who trespass against us; and lead us not into temptation; but deliver us from evil. Amen."

We Pray for Mercy
Jesus, You are the Lamb of God. On the Cross, and in this Mass, You offered Yourself to God for me. I beg You to keep me far away from all bad people, all bad places, and all bad things.

"Lamb of God, Who takes away the sins of the world, have mercy on me."

Put Your kinds arms 'round me,
    Feeble as I am;
You are my Good Shepherd,
    I Your little lamb.
Since You come, dear Jesus,
    Now to be my guest,
I can trust You always,
    Lord, for all the rest.

We Receive Jesus

I receive the Host. Then I go back to my place. I talk to Jesus. I think about Jesus in Bethlehem, and think of kneeling down there, holding the tiny Baby quite close against my heart. I say to Him,

"O Jesus dear, O Jesus dear,
    I am so glad to hold You here;
Although You are so weak and small,
    You are my God, and Lord of all.

O Babe divine, O Babe divine,
    Just for a little You are mine.
And I can press You to my heart,
    All great and holy as You art.

My Brother sweet, my Brother sweet,
    I kiss Your tender little feet,
And lay my face against Your cheek,
    And am too happy quite to speak.

Dear Infant Jesus, do not cry,
    For I will really, really try
Never to hurt You any more,
    Never to make Your sweet Heart sore.

O Jesus dear, O Jesus dear,
    I want to have You always near,
I want my little heart to be
    A soft, white cradle-bed for Thee."

I speak to our Lord in any little prayers I know. He does not need grand words. I tell Him I love Him. I tell Him I wish I could love Him more. I tell Him I am glad to be with Him. I give Him all I have. I want to please Him always, and never, never make Him sad.

I do not need to say all the prayers in this book. It is better to say a few slowly and think about what they mean than to say a great many in a hurry. Our Lord likes my own words best, But, if I cannot think of anything to say, I will read some prayers to Him and speak to Him from my heart.

We Receive God's Blessing
At the end of Mass, the priest makes the Sign of the Cross. He blesses us, saying, "May God, the Father, the Son, and the Holy Spirit, bless you. Amen."

"Dear Jesus,
We followed Your life through the Mass. Now, we are going home. We will think of You. We will soon visit You again in church. Please watch over us. Amen."

The Holy Sacrifice is done,
    Bless me, O Father, with the Son,
And Holy Spirit, Three in One,
    While never-ending ages run.

Bless me, before I go away,
    That all I think, or do, or say
May praise and please You every day
    And show I've been to Mass today.

After Mass
We say three Hail Marys.
Then we say, "Hail, holy Queen, Mother of Mercy; our life, our sweetness, and our hope. To thee do we cry, poor banished children of Eve. To thee do we send up our sighs, mourning and weeping in this valley of tears.

Turn then, most gracious advocate, thine eyes of mercy toward us; and after this our exile, show unto us the blessed fruit of thy womb, Jesus. O clement! O loving! O sweet Virgin Mary! Pray for us, O holy Mother of God, that we may be made worthy of the promises of Christ. Amen."

"St. Michael, the archangel, defend us in battle. Be our defense against the wickedness and snares of the devil. May God rebuke him, we humbly pray; and do thou, O prince of the heavenly host, by the power of God thrust into hell Satan and the other evil spirits who prowl about the world for the ruin of souls."

"Most Sacred Heart of Jesus, have mercy on us!" (This is repeated three times.)

I Pray the Sacraments

The sacraments were made by Jesus Christ to make us holy. Each sacrament gives sacramental grace, and sanctifying grace, which makes the soul pleasing to God.

All the sacraments have signs which can be seen, heard, or felt—like water, words, oil.

Baptism washes away original sin and makes us children of God. Penance takes away the sins committed after Baptism. Confirmation makes us soldiers of Jesus Christ. Holy Eucharist gives us Jesus Himself in the Holy Sacrifice of the Mass and in Holy Communion. Holy Orders gives us priests and bishops to care for our souls. Anointing of the Sick helps us when we are very ill. Matrimony gives us loving parents.

CONFESSION

Dear Jesus, I am going to confession.
I am going to tell my sins to the priest.
The priest will give me absolution for my sins.
He will make the Sign of the Cross over me.
This means that You, Jesus, forgive my sins.

The Sign of the Cross reminds me that You died because of my sins.
It also reminds me that You are hurt by sin. You suffered on the Cross. Dear Jesus, I am sorry I have sinned. Help me to make a good confession.

 Dear Jesus, I have six things to do to make a good confession.

First, I must ask the Holy Spirit to help me to know what my sins are.
Second, I must try hard to remember what sins I have committed.
Third, I must tell God that with all my heart I am sorry I have sinned.
Fourth, I must promise God that I will sin no more.
Fifth, I must tell my sins to the priest in confession.
Sixth, I must do the penance he gives me.

I Pray to the Holy Spirit

"Come, Holy Spirit. Come into my mind.
Come, Holy Spirit. Come into my heart.
You can give me the grace to know what sins I have committed.
You can give me the strength and the courage to confess my sins even though I may be afraid.
Give me the grace to know my sins.
Give me the grace to confess them honestly and without fear.
Holy Spirit, help me make a good confession.
Give me strength to be brave in the future. Amen."

I Examine My Conscience

Did I miss Mass on a Sunday or a Holy Day when I could have gone?
Did I laugh at Mass or did I play at Mass?
Was I late for Mass?
Did I use the Name of God without respect?
Did I disobey my father or my mother?
Did I fight or did I become angry (without a good reason?

I Talk with God

Did I annoy others?
Did I think or say or do anything impure?
Did I steal anything?
Did I tell a lie?

I Tell God I Am Sorry

Dear Jesus, I know that You will forgive my sins. But I know, too, that You will punish me for my sins.
When we do wrong, we must be punished. That is only fair.
I am sorry for my sins. I do not like to be punished for them.
But I have done wrong.
I know, Jesus, that sin hurts You. I know that it was because of sin that You suffered and died on the Cross.
I am sorry for my sins because my sins have hurt You, my Jesus.

"Dear Jesus, if I had been with You that dreadful night in the Garden, and seen how sad my sins had made You, I am sure I should have been sorry for them. Help me to be sorry now. I wish I had never done the things that made You sad. I will try not to do them again. Amen."

I Promise to Do Better

Dear Jesus,
I know how much my sins have hurt You.
I am sorry that I have hurt You.
I do not want to hurt You ever again.
I do not want to sin ever again.
How can I be sure of not hurting You?
I will try very hard never again to sin.

But You must help me, dear Jesus.
I cannot be good without Your help.
Help me, Jesus. I will try very hard to be good. This will show I love You.

I Confess to the Priest
I go quietly into the confessional. I kneel.
I tell the priest how long it has been since my last confession.
I tell him my sins.
I hide nothing from him.
I hide nothing from God.
I tell how many times I did each sin.
I tell the priest I am sorry for my sins.
If the priest asks me questions, I answer him honestly.
The priest gives me a penance.
I say the Act of Contrition. I thank the priest. I go out of the confessional.

I Do My Penance
I kneel before the Blessed Sacrament.
I do the penance the priest gave me.
My sins are forgiven.

O dear Jesus,
once again, You have forgiven me!
Once again you show me Your mercy and Your love.

I sinned against You many times.
But every time I go to confession, You forgive my sins.
Thank You, dear Jesus, for Your great mercy.
Thank You, dear Jesus, for Your great love.
Help me to love You more and more each day.

Prayer after Confession

O my crucified Jesus, I kneel at Your feet as a sinner. I have often offended You but I will do so no longer.

"O my God, since You willed to die for my sins, forgive me for them all. Help me, my Jesus, for I desire to become good and pleasing to You no matter what it costs. At the same time, help me that I may be able to do what You want. Amen."

Communion Prayers

Who is coming to me? Jesus is coming to me. My Lord and my God! You are coming to me in Holy Communion.

Long ago, You lived in the Holy Land. The children loved You, and You loved them. One day, mothers and fathers brought their children to You. They asked You to bless the boys and girls. You took each one in Your arms. You blessed each one. How happy they were! Oh, how those children must have loved you!

Our Best Friend

You are the best Friend of children. You are my best Friend. Jesus, I cannot see You. I see the Sacred Host. But I know You are really and truly there under what looks like bread.

"O my Lord and my God! You are coming to me in Holy Communion. Come soon. I need You, dear Jesus. With Your help, I can be good, and gain heaven. Help me, dear Jesus. I love You, and I want to stay near You always. Amen."

An Act of Faith

"Jesus, my God! I believe You are here in the Sacred Host. You will come to me in Holy Communion soon. You will then be really and truly here in my heart. I believe this because You said it. Amen."

An Act of Hope

"Jesus, my God! I know You will give me Your holy grace to make my soul pure. I know You will give me grace because You have promised it and You always keep Your promises. Amen."

An Act of Trust

"Most of all, I hope You will take me to live with You in heaven some day. Dear Jesus, I trust You because You are all good; You are all true. Amen."

An Act of Love

"Jesus, my God! I love You because You are all good, and You love me. You gave me all the good things I have. You want to make me happy now and in heaven. Amen."

An Act of Love

"You died on the cross to save me from sin. You opened the gate of heaven for me. You love me with all Your Sacred Heart. Help me to do kind acts to show my love for You. Amen."

An Act of Contrition

"Jesus, my God! I am sorry for my sins. I am sorry because I have offended You. But You suffered much. I am sorry because my sins hurt You on the Cross. Amen."

Receiving Holy Communion

When the time comes to receive Jesus in Holy Communion, I walk quietly to the front. I fold my hands.

When the priest or Eucharistic minister comes to me, I bow and then hold up my head. I open my mouth. I put my tongue on my lower lip. The priest lays the Host on my tongue. OR I bow and extend my hands (left placed over the right) so that the Host can be placed in them. I step to the side and make the Sign of the Cross.

I swallow the Host as soon as I can. I go back to my place. I kneel. I pray to Jesus. I thank Him.

Prayers after Holy Communion

"Jesus, my God, I thank You for coming to me. I thank You for all the good things I have. Most of all, I thank You for . . . I want to give You something to keep. I will give You my own self to be Yours always. Help me to act as You did when You were a boy. Help me obey my father and mother. Help me to be kind, at home, school and play. Help me think of acts to do for love of You. You did so much for me. Amen."

I Ask for a Favor

"Dear Jesus, I want to ask for many things. You are God and King. You can do everything. So You can give me what I am begging for. You are all good. You are all kind. You love me. So You will give me what I ask if it is good for me. You will say "No" if it is not good for me. Then, You will give me something better. Please, give me. . . I will thank You if You say "Yes" or "No." I trust in You. Amen."

Communion Thanksgiving
"Dear Jesus, I must go away now. It was good of You to come to me in Communion. Please, come often. I love You. Stay with me always. Do not go away. Then I can visit You often in my own heart. That is, I can make Spiritual Communions many times during the day. When I make a Spiritual Communion, I talk to You, dear Jesus, just as I do after I receive You in Holy Communion. I will try making many Spiritual Communions. Amen."

We Renew Baptismal Vows

Priest: "My dear children, our Lord is coming to you in Holy Communion. You know what He has done for you, and your hearts are filled with love for Him. Will you do something to show your love for God?"

Children: "Yes, Father. We will."

Priest: "You were babies when you were baptized; so, you did not know what God was doing for you, and you could not make the promises that we call the Baptismal Vows. Now you are able to do this. Your Godparents promised that you would be a Catholic. They made this promise for you. Then the priest could give you the holy Sacrament of Baptism even though you were little babies. God's wonderful gift of Baptism took away original sin and made you children of God. It opened the gates of heaven for you. It made you members of the Holy Catholic Church. It is your greatest gift. The Catholic Church is the mother of your souls. She will give you all the help you need to live a good life in this world and win the everlasting joys of heaven.

"The first promise is to renounce Satan. 'Renounce' means to have nothing to do with, to keep away from, to hate. God is your best Friend. He is all-good. He loves you. He tells you to be good so that you will keep out of sin, be truly happy, and go to heaven.

"Satan is your worst enemy. He is bad. He hates you. He tells you to be bad so that he can get you into sin, make you unhappy, and pull you down into the fire of hell. He wants to get your soul. Do you renounce Satan?"

Children: "We do renounce him."

Priest: "The second promise is to renounce Satan's works. Bad, mean, cruel, hateful, wicked things are the works of Satan. Do you renounce his works?"

Children: "We do renounce them."

Priest: "The third promise is to renounce Satan's pomps. His pomps are things he offers to give you if you will sin. They are a little bit like poisoned candy. It may look good or taste good, but it will make you sick, and it may kill you. Satan's pomps may look fine but they are soul poison. Do you renounce his pomps [empty promises]?"

Children: "We do renounce them."
Priest: "Catholics must believe all the truths that the

Church believes and teaches because God has made them known. Do you believe all the truths which the Holy Catholic Church believes and teaches?"

Children: "We believe them."

Priest: "My dear children, our Lord is pleased with you now. Keep your promises. Be true to the faith of the Holy Catholic Church. May God bless you."

Children: "Amen."

I Pray My Devotions

When you love someone, you want to be near him and to do little things to please him. This is called devotion. God is your best friend. Jesus, Who is God came to earth to live near you. He waits in the tabernacle for you to visit Him. Devotion to Jesus in the Blessed Sacrament will make you strong. Receiving Holy Communion pleases Jesus.

You can show devotion to Mary by saying her rosary, by wearing her scapular, and by being pure.

Show devotion to your angel who helps you.

The saints whose names you received in Baptism and Confirmation became your special friends.

The Way of the Cross

Dear Mother Mary, I know I can gain many indulgences if I make the Stations well. Help me to gain these indulgences:

- I can gain a partial indulgence for saying, "We adore You, O Christ, and we praise You, etc."
- I can gain a plenary indulgence for making the Way of the Cross in a Catholic church by myself or with the priest and the people.
- If I cannot visit all the Stations, I can gain a partial indulgence for each one I visit.

Before the Stations

Before I begin the Stations, I will make a good Act of Contrition. I will tell God how sorry I am that my sins made Him suffer. Before each Station, I will say this prayer: "We adore You, O Christ, and we praise You because by Your Holy Cross You have redeemed the world."

After each Station, I will say one Our Father and one Hail Mary.

"Dear Mother Mary, help me to say these prayers well. I can then show Jesus I am sorry for my sins. Amen."

A Prayer to Jesus
"Dear Jesus, You suffered very much when You carried Your heavy cross up the hill of Calvary. You suffered when the soldiers nailed You to Your Cross. You suffered for me. You suffered for all men. You knew that many people would love You. Dear Jesus, I love You. I know that You suffered because of sin. I am sorry that I hurt You by my sins. Now I will see how terrible sin is.

✝ First Station – Jesus Is Condemned to Death
Dear Jesus, Pilate knew You were a good man. But he told soldiers to nail You to a cross. Pilate was a coward. Help me to say "No" when I am tempted to sin. Help me to do right.

✝ Second Station – Jesus Takes Up His Cross
Dear Jesus, I have sinned. You suffered for me. You were crucified to save me from hell. Sometimes hard things happen to me. They are little crosses. Help me to take them well.

✝ Third Station – Jesus Falls the First Time
Dear Jesus, Your road was stony. You slipped and fell.

But You got up again. Sometimes I slip. I do something wrong. Help me get up again, as You did, and go on trying to be good.

✝ Fourth Station — Jesus Meets His Mother Mary
Dear Jesus, mean and cruel men beat You with whips and clubs. Sweet Mother Mary, You saw it all. You felt His pain. You came to comfort your own Son, Jesus. Help me to comfort Jesus.

✝ Fifth Station — Simon of Cyrene Helps Carry the Cross
Dear Jesus, the cruel men thought You would die on the way. They made Simon help You carry Your Cross. He saw how good You are, and he helped You. I will help You, too, by keeping out of sin.

✝ Sixth Station — Veronica Wipes the Face of Jesus
Dear Jesus, the Blood from the cuts was running into Your eyes. You could hardly see. Veronica ran to help You. She wiped the Blood away. I want to be like her. I will do kind acts for love of You.

✝ Seventh Station — Jesus Falls for the Second Time
Dear Jesus, Your cross was heavy. It was hard for You to carry it up the hill. But You kept on and on. Then, You fell again. Sometimes I fall into sin. Help me to get up again and go on.

✝ Eighth Station — Jesus Meets the Women of Jerusalem
Dear Jesus, some children and their mothers met You. They pitied You and began to cry. You comforted the

children and mothers. We comfort You, Jesus, by trying to be good.

✝ Ninth Station — Jesus Falls a Third Time
Dear Jesus, You were almost at the top of the hill of Calvary. You were very tired. You fell a third time. But You got up again. Help me not to give up, no matter how hard it is to be good.

✝ Tenth Station — Jesus Is Stripped of His Clothes
Dear Jesus, the cruel men took Your beautiful robe. They tore open all the cuts the whips made. You were taking my punishment for me. Help me to be kind. Help me to be unselfish.

✝ Eleventh Station — Jesus Is Nailed to the Cross
Dear Jesus, You let the cruel men drive nails into Your hands and into Your feet. You did this to show me how terrible sin really is. Help me be sorry. Help me, dear Jesus, to stay away from all sin.

✝ Twelfth Station — Jesus Dies on the Cross
Dear Jesus, You hung on the cross for three long hours. Finally, You died. You died to open the gates of heaven for me. O Jesus, I love You. Help me to do right. Help me to win heaven.

✝ Thirteenth Station — Jesus Is Taken Down from the Cross
Dear Jesus, after You died, Your friends took You down from the cross. Mother Mary washed away the Blood and dust. Dear Mother Mary, You loved Jesus so much. Help me to love Jesus.

I Talk with God

✝ FOURTEENTH STATION — JESUS IS LAID IN THE TOMB
Dear Mother Mary, you saw His holy Body put into the grave. But you knew that Jesus would rise again and come to you again. Dear Jesus, help me to receive You worthily in Holy Communion.

BENEDICTION

Dear Jesus, You are really and truly present on the altar. You are the King of kings, the King of heaven and the King of earth. You know all things. You can do all things. In Your heavenly home, the angels and saints crowd around Your throne. They sing Your praises. They sing their love for You.

But You want to be near us, even though we hurt You by our sins. You stay on the altar so we can adore You in church.

JESUS IN THE HOST

"O Jesus in the Sacred Host, I adore You. You died on the Cross to save me from sin. You opened the gate of heaven for me. But the devil does not want me to go in by that holy gate. He tries to get me to sin. O Jesus in the Sacred Host, help me win my fight. Help me to keep away from sin. Help me say "No" when I am tempted. Help me do many good acts to please You. Help me so that I may one day enter heaven and live with You forever. Amen."

O Jesus really hidden
    Within that Sacred Heart
Who heaven's gates has opened
    At such a bitter cost.

Fierce foes surround us daily,
  Lord, shield us with Your care.
From heaven's heights defend us
  And bring us safely there.

Prayer to the Trinity
"O Most Holy Trinity, God the Father, God the Son, God the Holy Spirit! You are all good. You are almighty. I kneel down before You. I praise You. I adore You. I love You. Bless me, dear God. Bless all of us here. Bless all who love You. Bless all who do not love You now. Amen."

The Divine Praises
"Blessed be God.
Blessed be His Holy Name.
Blessed be Jesus Christ, true God and true man.
Blessed be the Name of Jesus.
Blessed be His most Sacred Heart.
Blessed be Jesus in the most Holy Sacrament of the Altar.
Blessed be the great Mother of God, Mary most Holy.
Blessed be her holy and Immaculate Conception.
Blessed be her glorious Assumption.
Blessed be the name of Mary, virgin and mother.
Blessed be St. Joseph, her most chaste spouse.
Blessed be God in His angels and in His saints.
Amen."

The Rosary
When we say the rosary, we are talking to our Lady. As we pray, we think of the beautiful lives of Jesus

and Mary. We hope to see our Lady in heaven. Does anyone ever see her now on earth? Yes. But not often. Our Lady comes only when she has something great to tell her children.

One day, two girls and one boy saw our Lady. She appeared to them. She came to tell all of us to say the rosary well. The three children were Lucy, Jacinta, and Francis.

Our Lady Appears

The children were making a playhouse. Lucy and Jacinta were getting the stones. Francis was making the walls.

Then, flash! A light—big, bright, quick, like lightning! Lucy called, "Run! Run! We must go home. A big storm is coming." They ran down the hill. Flash! Flash! The bright light came. They stopped. Flash! Flash! Flash! The light was all around them. Then, they saw our Lady.

Our Lady's Prayer

Holy Mary, Mother of God, was standing on a soft white cloud above a bush. Her robe and veil were like sun on snow, pure and lovely. Her face was kind and lit by a gentle smile.

"Do not be afraid," she said. "I will not hurt you." Then our Lady told them many wonderful secrets.

She asked them to say the rosary every day, lovingly and well. We want to do it, too.

Many Ways to Pray

SAYING THE ROSARY

On the Cross, we say the Creed. On the big beads, we say the Our Father. On the little beads, we say the Hail Mary. On the chain after the ten Hail Marys we say the Glory Be to the Father.

These true stories are called "Mysteries." The five stories about the Holy Child Jesus are the Joyful Mysteries. The five stories about the life of Jesus are the Luminous Mysteries. The five stories about the sufferings and the death of Jesus are the Sorrowful Mysteries. The five stories about Easter and heaven are the Glorious Mysteries.

JOYFUL MYSTERIES

1. THE ANNUNCIATION

The angel told Mary that God wanted her to be His mother. Mary said she would do what God wanted. "Mother Mary, help me to be obedient, as you were."

2. THE VISITATION

Mary visited her cousin. Elizabeth honored Mary. But Mary said that the honor should be given to God and not to herself. "Mary, help me to give honor to God and not to myself."

3. THE BIRTH OF JESUS

Jesus was born in a stable at Bethlehem. "Dear Jesus, You suffered much for me. Now help me, dear Jesus, to do things to please You."

4. THE PRESENTATION OF JESUS

Soon Joseph and Mary took Jesus to the Temple to

present Him to God. The priest at the Temple gave thanks that he could see Baby Jesus. "Jesus, help me to remember that when I am in church, I am with you."

5. THE FINDING OF JESUS

Once, in Jerusalem, Mary and Joseph lost Jesus. Finally they found Him. He was in the temple teaching God's word. "Dear Jesus, help me to keep God's Word."

LUMINOUS MYSTERIES

1. THE BAPTISM OF JESUS

Jesus was baptized by John the Baptist in the Jordan River. Jesus did not need to get baptized but He wanted to show us the right thing to do. "Jesus, help me to always set a good example for others to follow."

2. THE WEDDING AT CANA

Jesus' friends were running out of wine at their wedding. He changed large jars of water into wine to save them from embarrassment. "Jesus, help me to always be kind and considerate of other people."

3. PROCLAMATION OF THE KINGDOM OF GOD

Jesus spent three years telling others about God and teaching them how God expects us to act. He wants all of us to be with Him in heaven. "Jesus, help me to teach others about You and to love You so much that I will never hurt You by my sins."

4. TRANSFIGURATION OF OUR LORD

Jesus took His friends up the mountain and allowed them to see Him in His gloried Body. They wanted to stay with Him on the mountain to give Him glory.

"Jesus, help me to give glory to You by my every thought, word, and action."

5. The Institution of the Holy Eucharist
Before He died, Jesus was sad to leave His friends. He left them a great gift—His Body and Blood in the Sacrament of the Eucharist. "Dear Jesus, help me to love you in the Eucharist and to receive You as often as I can."

Sorrowful Mysteries

1. The Agony in the Garden
The night before Jesus died, He went to a garden to pray. God sent an angel. The angel comforted Jesus. "Dear Jesus, when I am afraid, I shall ask God to help me."

2. The Scourging at the Pillar
The soldiers found Jesus in the garden. They took Jesus away. They beat Him. "Jesus, Jesus, help me to suffer bravely for You!"

3. The Crowning with Thorns
After scourging Jesus, the soldiers pushed a crown of sharp thorns into His Head. Then they laughed at Him. "Dear Jesus, help me be good when people laugh at me for being good."

4. Carrying the Cross
The soldiers gave Jesus a heavy cross to carry. Jesus had to carry His cross up a steep hill. "Suffering Jesus, You obeyed God's will. Help me to do God's will."

5. The Crucifixion

The soldiers nailed Jesus to His cross for all the crowd to see. "Dear Jesus, You suffered and died for my sins. Help me to be good and to avoid sin."

Glorious Mysteries

1. The Resurrection

Three days after Jesus died on the Cross, His friends went to His tomb. Jesus was not there. He had risen. "Dear Jesus, may I be with You forever in heaven."

2. The Ascension

After Jesus' Resurrection, His friends saw Him one day ascend into heaven. "Dear Jesus, you left us Your Body and Blood in Holy Communion. Thank You for this gift."

3. The Holy Spirit Comes upon the Apostles

Jesus knew His friends on earth would miss Him. Jesus asked the Holy Spirit to descend upon the souls of His friends. "Come, Holy Spirit."

4. The Assumption

Jesus loved His Mother Mary very much. He took her up into heaven, body and soul. "O Mary, Jesus is your Son. He does everything you ask. Please ask Him to help me."

5. The Coronation of Our Lady

Jesus wished to honor His mother in a special way. He called the saints together to see His mother crowned the Queen of Heaven. "Dear Jesus and Mary, may I see you one day in heaven."

THE SCAPULAR

After First Communion, the priest will enroll me in the scapular. He will bless my holy scapular. He will put it on me.

Then, I will have the right to wear the scapular. The scapular is like a badge. A badge shows that one belongs to something. My scapular shows that I belong to the Catholic Church, that I am under the special care of our Lady. Our Lady will get many special graces for me. She will watch over me.

A Scapular Prayer

Our Lady will give me special help because I am her own child. She is my heavenly mother,

"Dear Mother Mary, thank you for giving me special graces and special help. I will wear my scapular or my scapular medal always. I will try to have a special love for you. I will try to act as your child should. I will try to act as your Son, Jesus, did. I will try to be a good Catholic. I know you will help me do all this. Amen."

THE MIRACULOUS MEDAL

A Sister named Catherine loved our Lady. She lived in the convent. She was good and kind. You would love Sister Catherine. Our Lady loved her.

One day our Lady came to Sister Catherine. She held out her hands to Sister Catherine. A wonderful light came from our Lady's fingers. Around our Lady like a frame was this prayer: "O Mary, conceived without sin, pray for us who have recourse to Thee." You should know this prayer by heart.

A Miraculous Medal Prayer

A picture of our Lady and the prayer are on one side of the Miraculous Medal.

"Dear Mother Mary, I know that the light which came from your fingers means the graces you are always getting from God for me. I know, too, that you want me to pray to you for these graces. I will pray to you every day. After I am enrolled, I will always wear my Miraculous Medal. I will be true to you. I will prove my love. Amen."

The Hearts of Jesus and Mary

On the back of the medal is a big "M," a cross, and two hearts. The big "M" is for Mary. The cross makes us think of Jesus dying for us. The heart of Jesus has a crown of thorns. Mary's heart has a sword in it. This is to show us that Mary suffered for us.

When the priest enrolls me, I will wear the medal. I will belong to Mary. Mary will get holy graces for me every day. Every time I say the prayer, I can get a partial indulgence.

I Visit Our Lord

The church is big, so dim, so still,
Where Jesus stays all day;
But He is waiting there for me.
I'll slip inside and pray.

Jesus,
You love to see Your little friend

Come tiptoe through the door.
And every time I visit You
I want to love You more.

"Jesus, my God, I adore You here present in the Sacrament of Your love! Amen."

I Visit Our Lord

O Lord Jesus Christ, You are here in Your home on the altar. You are God the Son, all good and all holy. You know all things. You know me. You know my needs. You can do all things. You can help me. You will help me. My angel is with me. He is singing for You: "Holy! Holy! Holy! Lord God of heaven!" He is telling You how much he loves You. But You are waiting now for me to tell You how much I love You.

I Pray to Jesus

"Oh, sweet Jesus! I do love You. I love You with all my mind and heart, with all my body and soul. I love You. because You made me, because You died for me, because You help me, because You love me. Yes, dear Jesus, I believe You, I trust You, I love You. I beg pardon for those who do not believe, do not trust, and do not love. Dear Jesus, help me to believe, trust, and love You more each day. Amen."

To the Child Jesus

Lord Jesus Christ, You are true God. You are true Man, too. Once You were a child. You had friends. We know the names of four of the boys: James, Joseph, Simon, and Jude. We do not know the names of the girls. But these boys and girls were Your own cousins.

They loved You. They worked with You in St. Joseph's shop. They played with You in our Lady's garden. You helped them to be good and kind. You loved them very much.

Jesus' Friends

James, Jude, and Simon were Apostles. They lived for You. They died for You. Now, they are with You in heaven. They see You always. I cannot see You the way Your cousins did. I can have You in my soul in Holy Communion.

"Come soon, dear Lord. Come in Holy Communion. Be with me when I work. Help me to work for You. Be with me when I play. Help me to be kind to everybody as You were. Amen."

I Visit My Angel

I wish I could see the bright angel who stays all the
    day by my side.
I know I can say to him, "Thank you!" For being my
    guard and my guide.

O my angel! O holy angel of God! My beautiful friend! My wonderful friend! God sent you down from heaven to guard me.

"O angel of God, my guardian dear, be ever at my side. Amen."

I Talk to My Angel

O my angel! O holy angel of God! My beautiful friend! My wonderful friend! God sent you to guard me from bad people and from bad angels. God sent you to guide me and to help me find my way to heaven. God told you to take good care of me. You are with me all the days and all the nights.

You are with me now and always. You will stay with me all the time until I die.

I Pray to My Angel

"When I die, please take me to the holy gate of heaven if I have tried to be good. The gate will open for me. Oh, how happy you and Jesus shall be then! Dear angel, I want to be happy with Jesus forever in heaven. I know I can enter heaven only if I am good here on earth. Help me to be good. Help me to get to heaven. Jesus is waiting for me there. Jesus wants me to be in heaven with Him. And I want to be with Him. Amen."

Prayer for Holiness

Oh, how happy I shall be! Oh, how happy you will be; Oh, how happy Mother Mary will be! Oh, how happy Our Lord will be. O my holy angel, help me try hard to be good. I can find out what is right because: My mother will tell me. My father will tell me. The Church will tell me. I can do right because God will help me. God sent you to me. He wants you to help me.

"Dear angel, help me to do right. Lead me all the way up to God in heaven. Amen."

I Visit Our Lady

Virgin Mother full of grace,
    Hold me close to you.
Bring me often to your Son.
    Keep me pure and true.

Baby Jesus, smiling sweet
    On Your mother's knee,
I am opening wide my heart.
    Won't You come to me?

Mother Mary, keep my soul
    Pure from every sin,
So my holy Lord will smile
    When He does come in.

Bless me, Mary,
    Maiden mild,
Bless me, too,
    Her tender child. Amen.

I Visit Our Lady

O Blessed Virgin Mary, You are Jesus' Mother. Jesus is God. So you are the Mother of God. When you were living in Nazareth, a holy angel came to you. He asked you to be the mother of Jesus. God's Son wanted to come to earth. He wanted to have a soul and a body. Holy Mary, you gave Jesus a body like ours. You are Jesus' own dear mother. You are my mother, too. You are the holy mother Jesus gave to me.

I Ask Mary's Help

"Mary, Jesus gave you to me when He was on the Cross. You can help me because our Lord will do all that you ask Him. You will help me, dear Mother Mary, because you love me. Help me to know God. Help me to love God. Help me to serve God. Help me to be good. Help me to be kind. Help me to do right. I love you, Holy Virgin Mary, Mother of God. I will try to be good that I may live with Jesus and you in heaven forever and ever. Amen."

Why God Became Man

God the Son wanted to live in this world. He wanted to show us how to live right. He knew about all men. He even knew about me. He wanted to show me how to live for God, to work for God, to play for God, to pray to God. He wanted to show me how to win heaven. I cannot go to heaven if I have sins on my soul. So, He wanted to take my sins away. He wanted to die on the Cross to save me.

Jesus Gives Us Mary

Jesus wanted to die for me. But He wanted to stay here with me, too. He wanted to stay in the Blessed Sacrament. To do all this, God the Son needed a soul and a body. He needed a mother.

"Sweet Virgin Mary, you are Jesus' mother. From you, He has a body like ours. You are God's mother. You are my mother, too. Jesus gave you to me when dying on the Cross. I love you, Holy Virgin Mary, God's mother and mine. Help me to be good. Help me to love Jesus. Amen."

I Visit St. Joseph

"Dear St. Joseph, when you lived on earth, people did not know who you were. People thought you were just a carpenter. They did not know that you were the head of the Holy Family. They did not know that you were working for Jesus, the Son of God, and God's Holy Mother. Help me, St. Joseph, to work as you did. Help me to work for Jesus, to work for Mary, to love them both. Amen."

For Jesus and Mary

I want to work for Jesus and Mary. I know that I can work for them best by doing God's holy will. That is what Jesus and Mary want me to do. They want me to honor my parents, to obey my teachers, to be kind to my friends, to forgive my enemies, to be honest and truthful, to pray often. This is my work.

"St. Joseph, you worked so long for Jesus and Mary. Help me to work for them now. Amen."

I Obey

THE COMMANDMENTS OF THE CHURCH

The Church has made six very important laws. At the age of seven Catholic boys and girls must begin to keep these laws. They must attend Mass on Sundays and Holy Days of Obligation, eat no meat on Ash Wednesday and the Fridays of Lent (after age 14), go to confession at least once a year, receive Holy Communion during the Easter time, and make little sacrifices to help pay for the Church.

Later, when they want to marry they must keep the laws about marriage, and after eighteen, they must fast, that is, eat only one full meal on Ash Wednesday and Good Friday.

THE COMMANDMENTS OF GOD

God's commandments are built upon love—love God above all things and love your neighbor as yourself.

God loves you very much. He wants you to be happy with Him forever. He gave His Ten Commandments to help you get to heaven. The first three tell you what to do for God:

Do not have strange gods before Me.
Do not abuse the name of the Lord.
Keep holy the Lord's day.

The seven others tell what to do for yourself and your neighbor:

I Talk with God

Honor your father and mother.
Do not fight or kill.
Be pure in all actions.
Do not steal.
Do not tell lies.
Be pure in thoughts and desires.
Do not wish for things that belong to another.

The child who obeys these commandments of God will always be happy.

I Live in the World

God created the world and gave us many good things. He gave us this beautiful land of America and blessed it in many ways. God wants us to honor Him. He wants us to love Him. He wants us to serve Him.

GOD'S GIFTS TO US
God gave us His Son, Jesus, to be our Brother and Savior. He gave us His mother to be our mother. He gave us His Church to lead us to heaven.

OUR HOME
The most important group is the family. Everyone in the family has a right to be loved and to share in its work, joy, and sorrow. We must work and pray together.

God wants us to obey our parents. God wants us to get along with our brothers and sisters. He wants us to be kind to everyone.

OUR NATION
Long ago, many families joined together to make laws. They wanted everyone share God's gifts. This is how nations and governments began. God wants us to make good laws and to keep them.

He wants us to pray for our rulers and to obey them. He wants us to help and to protect our neighbors.

After the discovery of America many people came here. They wanted to be free to worship God. Many priests and sisters came to teach the people more about God.

Our Church
God asks us to serve Him. He wants us to talk to Him often. He expects us to be very attentive at Holy Mass.

Our School
There are many fine Catholic schools. Every Catholic child should try to go to a Catholic school. God wants us to learn all we can.

Our Companions
We all like to play. Every game has its rules. Games can help us to keep laws. Every girl and boy should be honest and fair.

I Love God

WALKING WITH OUR FATHER

There was a little child who was often taken by her father as his companion in his walks. The two loved each other dearly but he was a silent man, and so it often happened that they walked along hand in hand, for a long time without speaking.

Then, suddenly, the little hand felt a loving pressure, which meant, "My child, though I am silent, I am thinking of you and loving you."

At once both her little hands pressed hard the hand they held, which meant, "And, Father dear, I am thinking of you and loving you."

Now we are all like that little child. We are walking through this world by the side of our heavenly Father. We do not hear Him speak, except now and then low down in our hearts to tell us what we ought to do or not to do. But often, there is a silent pressure that shows us He is thinking of us.

Sometimes, it is a joyful surprise—Mother has given us a kitten that we wanted very much; or we have a lovely day for our picnic when we were afraid it was going to rain; or our toothache is better after a Hail Mary. But sometimes the pressure of our Father's hand is quite different from this. A great disappointment comes—a pouring day when we did so want it to be fine for our special day; or we get a scolding for spilling some milk; or someone was unfair to us at play.

Do these nasty things come from our heavenly Father too? Yes, everything comes from Him. Nice things and nasty things both help us to heaven, and so He lets troubles come as well as joys. If we use both as we ought—if we thank Him for what we like, and try to bear patiently what we don't like—*because He sends it,* this pleases Him more than we can say and gets us a great reward in heaven.

Some every brave people thank Him for the hard things too, because they are sure He knows best what is good for them. Can we be brave like this?

Was that little child afraid as she trotted along by her father's side, when a big fierce dog came up and looked at her, or when the great horned cows passed close by? No. Perhaps she held his hand a little tighter, and said, "Father, Father, take care of me!" but she was not afraid—*for he was there.*

And we need not be afraid of the cruel devil when he tries to hurt us by getting us to do wrong. He cannot *make* us to wrong when we do not want to do it. And we shall never want to do it; we shall never dare to do it if we remember God sees us always.

Our heavenly Father is close by us all day long and all night through, when things try us in the day time and we are getting angry, when we are in the dark in our bed at night. He is always there close by, taking care of us, ready to help us. If the devil comes to tempt us and we say, "Father, take care of me," He will drive the devil away. He loves to hear His little child cry to Him like this when there is danger near.

Working for Our Father

Another thing I want to tell you about this little child and her father. She used often to do things to please him. They were not very grand things, you may be sure, but you should have seen how much he made of them, and the beautiful things he gave her in return.

Sometimes she thought of these presents and worked hard to get them. And sometimes—because she loved her father dearly—she did not think of presents at all, but only of pleasing him whom she loved. And sometimes when she brought him work she had done, and waited for the reward, and said, "Dear Father, aren't you going to give me anything for it?" he would say, "But, my child, this was not done to please me—now was it? It was done to please yourself, and you never thought of me at all." Then she would hang down her head and be ashamed, and think she would not work to please herself again.

Our heavenly Father likes us, His children, to work for Him, that He may be able to give us a great reward some day. He will reward the least thing we have done for Him—even a cup of cold water given for His sake. Whether we eat or drink, or whatever we do—our schoolwork, our play, things we like, things we dislike—we may offer all to Him, and so earn a great reward in heaven. This is why we say in our Morning Prayers:

"O Jesus, through the most pure heart of Mary, I offer You the prayers, work and sufferings of this day for all the intentions of Your Divine Heart." *Or*

"My God, I offer You this day,
All I think, or do, or say,
Uniting it with what was done
On earth by Jesus Christ Your Son."

And not only when we wake in the morning and at our Morning Prayers, but often during the day should we lift our hearts to God in some little prayer:

"O my God, I offer You my heart and my soul."

"My Jesus, mercy."

"Heart of Jesus, in You I trust."

"Jesus, meek and humble of heart, make my heart like unto Your Heart."

Before beginning anything, pray:
"My God, I do this for the love of You."

In temptation, pray:
"Lord, save us, we perish."

In sickness or in pain, pray:
"Lord, Your Will be done; take this for my sins."

"Father, not my will, but Your will be done."

These are the pressures of our heavenly Father's hand that shows Him His little child is thinking of Him and loving Him.

Working for God helps us to work *well*. If we remember He is always by, watching to see how we do what we are doing *for Him*, we will be ashamed to give Him what is badly done. We must try to give Him our very best. We may offer our work for any of our Lord's intentions, which means the things He wants—for the dying, that they may get safe to heaven, for poor sinners, or for the poor waiting souls in Purgatory, who are always looking at the big gates to see if their good angel is coming to let them out, always wondering if some kind child is thinking of them and saying some short prayer, or doing some good work to help them in their pain.

We may think of the reward God will give us for what we do for Him, and He likes us to think of it. Our Lord tells us not to work just to get praise, or prizes or presents from others, though we may want to get these too. But to try to deserve a reward from our Father who is in heaven. Or to do our work or to bear our pain just to please Him. This is what He likes best of all. This gives Him a joyful surprise. Do things sometimes *just to please Him*.

If often during the day, and whenever we are tempted to think or say or do anything wrong, we remember that God is there, watching to see if we are going to behave like dear good children, we shall never do any big sin. He tells us so Himself.

And if we do all our work to please Him, and thank Him for all that happens to us, whether we like it or not, saying whatever comes, "Thanks be to God!"—why, then we are doing what the saints do!

It is this than makes people saints. Children can be saints and very dear to God as well as grown-up people; there have been many children saints.

Now we know what to do. Shall we not try to be saints? God loves those who try.

Meditation

from
A Week of Communions

by
"Lamplighter"

Verses by
V. E. C.

Meditation

To the Boys and Girls
Who Use These Meditations

This is not a Preface, something separate from the book itself. It may not be skipped because it explains how these meditations came to be and how they are to be used.

Among the many boys who made the sacrifice of their lives and were killed in World War I was one whose name was John. He enjoyed life thoroughly but was always very good in a quiet, unassuming way, and very lovable. When he was nine, he went to the elementary school, and then up to the high school of which it is a part, and then to college. He spent three years at the college whose name is Corpus Christi—the Body of Christ—and whose coats of arms show the pelican feeding its young with its own blood—which is a type of our Lord feeding our souls with His own Body in Holy Communion.

John had a successful career both at school and at college; and when the war broke out, he joined up immediately, not because he really wanted to be a soldier but out of a sense of duty. He made a very fine soldier, however, and soon got his captaincy. His men loved him because he was always kind and thoughtful, and very plucky when there was danger. After eight months of active service, in one of his letters to his mother, he said, "We have been in rest billets in a village which is so situated that life goes on as though there were no war. It is down in a hollow, quite out of the world, and the little church is always open. I have been lucky enough to have a *week of Communions*."

That letter was written a few days before John's death, and those who knew him felt that the week of Communions, so near the fighting line, was a special grace of God to reward him for his love and fidelity to Holy Communion during all his short life. When John was hit, one of his brother officers—not a Catholic—fetched a priest for him to give him the Last Sacraments.

"Though we didn't think he was going to die, we thought we ought to get the padre because John was so keen on his religion."

That was what they wrote to his mother after he died.

This little book is dedicated to his memory and is written with the hope that the boys—and the girls too—who use it, may be helped to be "keen on their religion" and have many a week of Communions in their lives, because going to Holy Communion is both the *cause* and the *effect* of this "keenness" about religion, and the best means of keeping near to God, which is what we all must do if we want to save our souls and, when this life is over, go to be happy with Him forever in heaven.

The stories from the Scriptures which follow—one for each day of the week—are chosen for you to think about in preparing for Holy Communion. The prayers that come after them are only *examples* of ways in which you can choose an incident from the Gospel and make up prayers about it for yourselves. Prayers right from our own minds and hearts are the most *real,* and the best place to find the thoughts for them is our Lord's life, which has in it all that we need to

Meditation

help our souls. Books like this little one are, then, written just to start you on your own prayer-making.

The verses are meant to be learned by heart. They are very simple, so you will not find that difficult, and they should be said at odd times during the day—not necessarily in church, nor even on your knees, but quietly to yourselves, now and again, as you go about, to keep the thought of your morning Communion in your mind, just as the notes of a tune running in your head remind you of a piece of music you have heard. A few plans, or outlines, of how to make the little meditations and prayers for *yourselves* are given in Parts II and III. The *Adoro Te* is on pages 111-113. Some of you can probably say it in Latin. For those who cannot, there is also a simple paraphrase in English of this most beautiful of all prayers to our Lord in the Blessed Sacrament. As most of you know, it is by St. Thomas Aquinas, who knew more about the Holy Eucharist than perhaps any other saint.

Many of you, when you go to Holy Communion, like to think of our Lord as a boy. These stories will help you to think out for yourselves how He would have spoken and acted at Nazareth. Ask Him to help you to become more like the kind of young person that He was.

Meditation

Jesus Teaches Me How to Talk with God: Seven Scenes from Our Lord's Life

1. OUR DAILY BREAD[3]
Our Lord once told the people that the best prayers were not very long ones, like those the heathens said. "*They* think that they will be heard because of their many words." He said that *we* were *not* to think that, and then He taught them quite a short prayer: the Our Father.

Another day when Jesus was quite alone praying, the Apostles came to Him. They waited until He had finished, and then they asked Him to teach *them* to pray. There must have been something about the way Jesus prayed that made them somehow feel that their own prayers were not much good. And once again our Lord repeated, "When you pray, say . . ." and then He went through the words of the Our Father.

Jesus, I think I understand. You meant that it is not the length of the prayer that we say that makes You listen to it, but what we say and how we say it. Your own prayer—the Our Father—is not long, but it asks for all the things that really matter: That You may be known and loved and served, and to have *first* place in our hearts even now on earth; that we may have grace to do Your will—that is, anything we know You *want* us to do; that we may forgive others so that You may forgive us; that You will give us grace not to give

---

[3] St. Matthew 6:5-15

in to temptation; that You will keep evil from us, especially the only real evil—sin.

But when I go to Communion, I like best of all to think of the words, "Give us this day our daily bread," because they do not only mean, "Give us food for our bodies"—but they mean even more, "Give me yourself daily." Come daily into my heart in Holy Communion because that will keep me from committing grave sin better than anything. I need food to keep life in my body; I need *You* to keep life in my soul. It is not hard, Jesus, to go to Communion every day at Catholic school: it is harder in the days of vacation, and perhaps it will be harder still when I am older. Please let me get into a habit now of going daily to You, so that I shall go on, if possible, doing it always.

"John" did not know he was to die so soon after that "week of Communions." He must have been very happy, though, when he *did* die, that during his life he had been kept good through Holy Communion and so was ready for death.

Mary, Mother, say often to Jesus for me, "Give him this day his daily Bread"—and St. John say it. too, please, for me, and for all my friends, "Give them this day their daily Bread." Amen.

> Jesus, come each morn to be
> Living Bread to nourish me,
> You are strong, and I am weak;
> Health and strength from Thee I seek.

Meditation

2. FISHERS OF MEN[4]

It was very early in the morning and our Lord was walking alone by the Sea of Galilee. He had come out to find His first helpers in His work, His first Apostles. He knew that they would be doing their ordinary job —fishing in the waters of the lake. Simon Peter was casting his nets when our Lord passed and so was Andrew, Peter's brother, and they must have been surprised by our Lord's words, "Come after me, and I will make you fishers of men." Perhaps they did not quite know what He meant, but just felt that they must follow Him, so they left their nets that very minute and went with Jesus.

A little further on our Lord saw a boat pulled up on the beach. It belonged to a man called Zebedee, and he was sitting in it with his two sons, James and John, and some men that he had hired to help, and they were all mending fishing nets. Our Lord said that He wanted *them* to come with Him too, and they left their father and the boat and everything and followed Jesus at once with Peter and Andrew.

I am not old enough, Lord, to be a "fisher of men" in the way you wanted the Apostles to be—really helping You in Your work of getting hold of men's souls and teaching them what to do with their lives, so as to get to heaven in the end. The only thing I can do *now* is to follow You by doing my best to please You each day and so, by degrees, becoming more useful to You. I have Holy Communion to help me, which those four fishermen had not. They were just doing their daily

---

[4] St. Matthew 4:18-22; St. Mark 1:16-20

tasks, but they must have done them well, in the way You wanted, for You to have called them to do bigger things.

Help me, Jesus, in Holy Communion to do my work well—not to be slack in lessons or games (It is harder at lessons.), so that I may be counted someday among Your friends who really help You.

I do not want just to keep out of grave sin. I want to show You that I am grateful for all You do for me by the way I try not to commit even small sins.

Please, our Lady, help me to be faithful to Holy Communion and to prepare for it by spending my day as well as I can.

St. John, pray for me. You were not always a saint and You know how hard it is sometimes to do what is right. When you followed our Lord that morning you were just an ordinary fisherman, but He turned you into an Apostle, a fisher of men. Ask Him to do that with me.

> Lord, to be a "fisherman"
> I am too small, and lowly;
> But while Your priests are out at sea,
> I can do some work for Thee
> By trying to be holy.

3. An Evening of Miracles[5]

Our Lord had spent a very busy day, and when, at sunset, He came out through the door of Simon's little house He found the narrow street full of sick

---
[5] St. Matthew 8:16-17; St. Mark 1:32-34; St. Luke 4:40-41

Meditation

people all waiting for Him. It looked as though the whole town had turned out and was gathered round the door.

Some of those in the crowd were possessed by devils, and Jesus, with just a word, cast them out. The evil spirits began calling out, "You are the Son of God." They realized that He was God and that His power was much greater than theirs, and they were angry at having to go away and leave in peace the poor creatures whom they had got into their clutches. Our Lord touched every one of the sick people, and at once they were well again.

The prophet Isaiah, who lived hundreds of years before our Lord, said many things about Him which were so true that he might have been writing after they had happened instead of so long before. One thing came true *many* times in our Lord's life—among others, the scene we are thinking of in the street at Capernaum, "He took away our infirmities and bore our diseases."

When we are preparing for Holy Communion, *we* are like that crowd waiting for the door to open and for Jesus to come out, only it is the door of His own house in the church—the tabernacle—and we are going to ask Him to cure not illnesses of the *body,* but of the *soul*.

When those who are sick are waiting at Lourdes for our Lord to pass in the processsion of the Blessed Sacrament, they keep on praying to Jesus to cure their blindness, and their deafness, and their lameness, and lots of other things, as the people in our Lord's life did, and in my Communion today, I will pray as they do—

"Jesus, let me see!"—see Your goodness to me, and Your patience with me, and then see my faults—my laziness and greediness, and untruthfulness and bad temper—and all my other faults, especially . . . (Here mention one that you are often told of and that you want very much to be sorry for and to correct.)

"Jesus, let me walk!"—along the road that leads to You, not stumbling along anyhow, and grumbling when the going is a bit hard; but being sporting, and stepping out, and making the best of it.

"Jesus, let me hear"—Your voice in my heart, telling me what to do to please You, what *not* to do so as to avoid displeasing You. I need strength for all this, but You will give it.

Our Lady of Lourdes, pray for me. It is much worse —if I could only understand it—to be blind, and deaf, and lame in my soul than in my body. You do understand that, so please help *me* to.

St. John, you were our Lord's best friend, so your prayers are good ones. Say some to Jesus for me that I may see what God wants of me, and hear His voice in my heart and make haste along the road that goes to heaven.

> At eventide when Jesus came,
> He cured the sick, the blind, the lame;
> And in this Sacrament Divine
> His healing hands are laid in mine
> I press them to my poor, weak soul:
> O, Jesus, Lord, please make *me* whole!

Meditation

4. CLIMBING A TREE[6]

His name was Zaccheus, and he was rich and a publican, the chief of them, a kind of superintendent of the tax-gatherers.

He had heard a lot about our Lord and wanted very much indeed to see Him, and so he joined the crowds on the road along which one day Jesus was to pass. But there were tall men in front of him, and he could not see a thing; so he climbed into a sycamore tree to have a good view. To his surprise, our Lord looked up as He passed under the tree, and saw Zaccheus and called up to him, "Zaccheus, come down quickly, because today I must stay at your house." Zaccheus was simply delighted and got down as fast as he could, and took Jesus to his house and gave a dinner-party in His honor. When the crowd saw Zaccheus going off with our Lord they grumbled, because they hated tax-gatherers anyway, and besides Zaccheus was not a very good man, and they thought our Lord ought not to be the guest of a man who was a sinner. But he was sorry, and did not want to go on being a sinner, and he told our Lord that he would give half of what he had to the poor, to make up for his sins, and that if he had cheated a man out of anything he was ready to give him back four times as much.

The reason why Jesus went to his house was because He wanted to help Zaccheus out of his bad life into a good one, and Jesus said so, in the words, "The Son of Man has come to seek and to save what was lost."

I think that the first thing that pleased our Lord

---

[6] St. Luke 19:2-10

about Zaccheus was his climbing up the tree to see Him. He cannot have liked doing it much, with all those people looking on, because he was not a boy, but a rather well-known man, and the crowd perhaps laughed at him. But he did not mind. Then Jesus did very big things for him, in return, first by making him sorry for his sins, and then by forgiving him. There is nothing more about him in the Gospels, but I am sure he turned out well and became one of our Lord's followers.

Jesus, You always reward those who do something for You, and You give much better things to us than we can possibly give to You. I do not like being laughed at, at least not always. Not when it is for doing something that I think is right, but that other people think is silly, or that it does not matter. There may be more things like that when I am older, but I count on You for help to do them. Very often You say to me, "Come down quickly because I want to come into the house of your soul to make you better," and, through laziness, I do not always receive You. Before I "come down," I have to "get up," and that is the hard part. Help me to value Holy Communion more than I do—to take the trouble, to put myself out, in order to receive You into my house.

Mary, Mother of God, who from the very beginning always did what He asked of you, help me to do what is right, especially about going often to Holy Communion.

St. John, to whom our Lady so often went to receive her Son under the disguise of the White Host, I come

Meditation

to you too. Help me by your prayers not to let laziness keep me from Holy Communion.

> I wish I had been Zaccheus
> On the branch of the sycamore tree;
> I wish our Lord had smiled, and said:
> "My child, come down to Me."
> Yet ev'ry day, if I did but think,
> When I'm warm and snug in bed,
> Our Lord calls up in His friendly voice:
> "Come down for your Daily Bread!"

5. A STORM AT SEA[7]

Our Lord noticed one evening that the Apostles seemed tired. He was tired too, so, seeing a great crowd beginning to collect, He thought that just for once He and His Apostles would escape from the people and get across to the other side of the Lake of Galilee.

He sent the crowd away and sailed across the water with His friends. He was so tired that He fell fast asleep, and the Apostles put a pillow under His Head to make Him more comfortable. They had not gone far before a storm began, and the wind blew harder and harder, and the waters grew rougher and rougher, until the boat began to fill with water and was in danger of sinking.

And all the time, our Lord slept on.

At last the Apostles were really frightened and went and woke Jesus, crying out to Him to save them.

---

[7] St. Matthew 8:23-27; St. Mark 4:35-41; St. Luke 8:22-25

I Talk with God

They seemed to think that He did not mind if they were drowned. But He *did,* and He never meant them to drown.

He stood up and said to the Apostles, "Why are you terrified, O you of little faith?" And to the waters He said, "Quiet! Be still!" and at once the wind dropped and the lake was quite calm again. Then, the Apostles began to whisper to one another, "Who then is this, who commands even the winds and the sea, and they obey him?" And again, they were afraid, not about the storm this time, for that was over. Their fear now was of another kind, because they began to understand that it must be God Himself Who was with them, though He only *looked* like the Carpenter of Nazareth, a poor man, like one of them.

Only little by little, Jesus, did Your friends come to know Who You really were. This story shows that. And even when they knew, they only saw God in You through *faith,* just as I do when You come to me in Holy Communion under the form of bread.

I *cannot* be afraid of You, my God, when You come like that, and I think that is why You have chosen to hide your Glory under something so simple.

I must then, Jesus, never fear You, even though I know that when I receive You I receive the Great God into my heart—a loving heart, but not a *holy* one, like the saints' hearts. Make me a tiny bit holier each time You come.

Mary, Mother of Jesus and of me, obtain for me a little of *your* faith and trust in our Lord.

Meditation

St. John, you who were in that boat, and at first were afraid, help me to learn from this story to have great trust in Jesus, and when I find it hard to be good, and that something like a storm is going on inside me, show me how to hold on to Jesus and be sure that He will not desert me. For, the devil's strength is nothing compared to our Lord's, I know that, and the devil cannot *make* me do wrong, so when he raises a storm by tempting me to sin I must not be frightened. Our Lord does not want me to be "drowned," and the devil has to obey Him, just as much as the winds and the sea had, so the boat of my soul is quite safe, especially if Jesus often comes into it in Holy Communion.

> My tiny boat is on life's sea,
> But Christ our Lord is close to me;
> He sleeps, yet at my cry of fear
> Will wake and whisper, "I am near."

6. Sowing Seed[8]

Wherever our Lord went, crowds seemed to follow Him. One day, when He was sitting on the seashore, more and more people came around Him, until at last He got into a boat and pushed out a little and talked to the crowd from there. Perhaps, looking up, He saw a man in the distance sowing seed, and that gave Him the idea of telling the parable of the sower who sowed his seed in four different kinds of soil. Some of the seed fell on a path, and of course the birds swooped

---

[8] St. Matthew 13:1-23; St. Mark 4;1-20; St. Luke 8:4-15

down and ate it all up at once. Some seed got scattered over rocky ground, with only a light covering of earth, so that its roots were not deep enough for it to do well, and it soon withered. Part of the grain fell among thorns, and as it grew the thorns grew too, and in the end choked it. But the sower sowed a good part of his seed in really rich earth, and it produced a splendid crop.

Afterwards when our Lord was alone with the twelve Apostles, they came and asked Him to explain the parable to them, as they had not understood it very well. He said that the seed is God's word to men, sown in their hearts, and that some men's hearts and minds are like the "path" where the things of God never really get into them at all, because they let the devil snatch them away from them at once. And other people are like rocks with a light covering of earth, quite pleased at first to hear God's teaching, but not *deep* enough for it to take root for long, and quickly put off by sufferings, or trouble, so that the growth is soon stopped.

The "thorny ground" means characters that are easily taken away from God and His service by their surroundings; business, riches, and pleasure soon absorb all their interest, and leave no room for God.

The "rich soil" the Apostles must surely have understood! Our Lord said it meant men who really *want* to hear God's word and carry it out, and who try very hard to do so, and, according to *how* hard they try, they produce good deeds, which if represented by figures would be like thirty, or sixty, or even a hundred.

Meditation

My dear Lord, in every Communion that I make, help me to become better and better "ground."

Let me not be the "path" kind of character, so uninterested and inattentive that words about God, and His will for me get carried off by the devil almost before I have heard them. I do not want to be like the "rocky ground" either—only serving You well for a short time, or when it is quite easy and everyone helps me, and no one hinders me. I do not want just to be good with good people and bad with bad ones, but to do what I think is right myself, in any kind of surroundings.

It must be more difficult for seed to grow among thorns than almost anywhere, for You said, Jesus, that the "thorns" meant things like riches and pleasure which nearly everyone loves. What I have to do is not to allow the things I like to get too strong a hold on me, not to be *too* keen about them—especially if they prevent me from keeping Your Commandments and practicing my faith.

I cannot do this by myself. I need Your grace. Please show me which of the three *bad* kinds of ground is most like my heart, so that I may try hard *not* to be that kind, and at every Communion look and see how the "seed" is wetting on, and make it grow well.

Mary, Mother of Jesus, You who from the very beginning were "good ground," like a lovely garden where the seeds are always flowering, pray for me.

St. John, you who heard our Lord explain this parable, pray for me too, that I may understand it and *do* the things it teaches.

My Father is the farmer
Who sows His seed divine.
My heart receives it from His hand,
So I can call it mine;
And by His very words, I'm told
Of seed that gave a hundredfold;
Work on, my soul, and never cease,
For it's God Who gives the increase.

7. THE UNGENEROUS MAN[9]

Walking one day with His disciples, Jesus was stopped by a man who ran up, and then knelt down before Him, saying, "Good teacher, what must I do to inherit eternal life?" Our Lord made rather a strange answer, "Why do you call me good? None is good but God alone."

Probably the man did not know that Jesus was God. Our Lord had told the disciples that they were not to go about telling people that He was the Christ, and He did not do it Himself—He wanted the Jews to come to that knowledge gradually, so He just gave this man an answer that would make him think.... Then He told him that the way to go to heaven was to keep the Commandments, and at once the young man said he had kept them all since he was a child, and he asked another question, "What do I still lack?"

Jesus *loved* him for keeping the Commandments so well. The Gospel says so—"looking at him, [He] loved him," and He was delighted that he wanted to do all he possibly could for God, so He replied, "There is still one thing left for you: sell all that you have

---

[9] St. Mark 10:17-31; St. Matthew 19:16-30; St. Luke 18:18-30

Meditation

and distribute it to the poor, and you will have a treasure in heaven. Then, come and follow me."

The end of the story is rather sad. When the man heard this answer, he felt he simply could not give up all he had to the poor, because he was very rich and wanted to keep his money, so he did not say a single thing more, but just went sorrowfully away.

Dear Lord, I *often* break Your Commandments, so I wonder if You ever look on *me* and love me. I do hope so, because I *try* when I have been to confession to begin again, and not commit so many sins.

I think this story is one that has in it lots of things to think about. We can see from it that You are pleased when people try hard to be good, and still more pleased when they want to do more for You than just what they are obliged. And also, that everything we give up for Your sake You remember, and will give us something much better in heaven. It was a pity that that man was not willing to do what You asked, when he seemed at the beginning to be so true. It is the same with me, I know. Sometimes I feel I want to do my very best, and then when it means giving up something I want, I turn around, and *do not*. That man had never made even *one* Communion, so he had not the help from You that I have.

Each time You come to visit my soul, put into it some courage, and generosity, and the desire to be a really *good* Catholic, now and still more later on—to stick to my prayers, and Mass and Communions, and so be ready for any sacrifices that You may want of me during my life.

I Talk with God

Our Lady, help me to serve Your Son well. You must know better than anyone how pleased He is when I want to do more than just to keep out of grave sin. I would like to do better than that in return for all He has done for me.

St. John, you were not a rich man like this one, but all the same you gave up all you had, and went and helped our Lord as well as you possibly could all your life. You were "the disciple whom Jesus loved," and I am sure you would like our Lord to have many more disciples whom He loves. Ask that I may be one.

> I'm sorry that the rich young man
> Turned back and answered "No."
> So, Lord, I will do all I can
> To follow where You go.
> It may be hard to give up things
> I want so much to do,
> But when You ask me, Lord, You know
> I'll give them all to You.

Meditation

I Talk with God
In Holy Communion

When you go to Holy Communion, always remember to pray for others—the Church, your parents, those who teach you, the poor, the sick, the suffering, your relatives and friends. There is no better prayer to say for all these than the one which the priest says in the Mass, before the Consecration. Here it is:

> Remember, Lord, your servants N. and N. and all gathered here, whose faith and devotion are known to you. For them, we offer you this sacrifice of praise or they offer it for themselves and all who are dear to them, for the redemption of their souls, in hope of health and well-being, and paying their homage to you, the eternal God, living and true.

Pray also for the dead. There may be souls very dear to you suffering in Purgatory and your prayer for them at Mass and Holy Communion will help them to get to heaven. Soon after the Elevation in the Mass, the priest says the following prayer for the faithful departed. Say it, or any other, for the Holy Souls:

> Remember also, Lord, your servants N. and N., who have gone before us with the sign of faith and rest in the sleep of peace. Grant them, O Lord, we pray, and all who sleep in Christ, a place of refreshment, light, and peace. (Through Christ our Lord. Amen.)[10]

---

[10] Texts from the *Roman Missal, Third Edition*, 2011, Eucharistic Prayer I

I Talk with God

Before you leave the church, say the following indulgenced prayer:

Behold, O kind and most sweet Jesus, I cast myself on my knees in Your sight, and with the most fervent desire of my soul, I pray and beseech You that You would impress on my heart lively sentiments of faith, hope and charity, with true repentance for my sins, and a firm desire of amendment, while with deep affection and grief of soul I ponder within myself and mentally contemplate Your five most precious wounds; having before my eyes that which David spoke in prophecy of You, O Good Jesus, ""They pierced My Hands and My Feet; they have numbered all My Bones."

Say one Our Father, Hail Mary, and Glory be to the Father for the pope and the Church.

Meditation

The Gospels Teach Me How to Talk with God: Seven More Scenes from Our Lord's Life

MAKING PRAYERS FOR OURSELVES

We have to *learn* how to pray, as we learn other subjects. First we are taught, or shown something, and then we have to go on studying and working and finding out more for ourselves.

Seven scenes from our Lord's Life have been set before you, and then a prayer, and a verse for you to say. The number "seven" was chosen so as to have different thoughts and prayers for each day of a week of Communions. Here are seven more scenes which you can find in the Gospels for yourselves. The prayers and verses, too, you must "make up."

1. THE MAN WHO CARED FOR A WOUNDED TRAVELER[11]
Notice that our Lord told a whole story in answer to the question, "Who is my neighbor?" He might have answered, "Everyone!" But He said it in a much more interesting way, to impress the law of charity on us all. Pray to be kind to others as often as you get the chance. Ask our Lord at Holy Communion to give you some chances today, and to help you to *take* them. Ask Our Blessed Lady for this too.

2. ONE GRATEFUL AND NINE UNGRATEFUL LEPERS
St. Luke was a doctor; perhaps that is why this story of the dreadful illness of leprosy had a special interest

---

[11] This story is only told in St. Luke 10:25-37.

I Talk with God

for him; anyway he is the only evangelist who tells it (St. Luke 17:11-19).

Leprosy makes the body hideous, but not half so hideous as sin makes the soul. Pray at every Communion that you may never commit a grave sin.

Evidently, prayers of thanksgiving please our Lord. He practically said so in this story. Do we *ask* more often than we *thank*? Or when we *get,* do we *forget* to thank? Ask our Lady to obtain for you the grace to thank God as she did, for all "the great things" He has done for you.

3. About a Long, Proud Prayer and a Short Humble One[12]

The Pharisee who bragged, even when he prayed, went home not "justified," our Lord said, when He spoke of him. The man thought himself just, but God did not. The poor publican was a sinner, but because he was humble, and sorry, our Lord forgave him, and made him "just": "I tell you, the latter went home justified rather than the former, for everyone that exalts himself shall be humbled, and the one who humbles himself will be exalted."

Pray at Holy Communion not to think yourself better than other people. You owe everything you have to God, so do not be proud if you are better at studies or at games or anything else than others; but grateful, and humble, like the man near the door who made a good prayer for us all to say, "O God, be merciful to me a sinner."

---

[12] St. Luke 18:9-14

Meditation

4. The Workmen Who Grumbled[13]

Think well over this story, because if you read it carelessly it seems, at first, as if it was *not* fair of the master of the vineyard to give as much money to the laborers who had only worked for one hour, as to those who had worked all day. But they had agreed in the morning about the amount of money they were to receive in the evening, and so what they were really complaining of was not the master's injustice to them, but his generosity to the latecomers. In other words, they simply were jealous. The master must have had some good reason for paying the last to come as much as the first. Probably they had labored harder and done much better work in their one hour than the others, who, perhaps, wasted the day away and did their job badly.

Make up a prayer asking Jesus in this Communion to keep you from the horrid sin of jealousy, or to help you to correct it if you do commit it, and to give you grace always to put your whole strength into all you do to please Him, so that whether your life be long or short He will be as good to you when it ends as He was to those workers in His vineyard.

5. The Alabaster Flask[14]

The story of this woman (It is thought that she was the one who was to become St. Mary Magdalen.) is a most encouraging story for every single one of us. She had committed many sins, but that did not make her

---

[13] St. Matthew 20:1-16
[14] St. Luke 7: 36-50

afraid of going to our Lord. She was sorry for them from the bottom of her heart, and she was forgiven because she showed "great love."

The alabaster box, full of precious ointment, which she broke over our Lord's feet, was a sign or symbol of the love and of the sorrow that poured out of her broken heart. Our Lord's parting words to her were, "Your faith has saved you; go in peace."

Pray today that no sin, however great it may seem to you, may ever cause you to lose your faith and trust in God's love for you, and His readiness to pardon you. You too have an "alabaster flask," a heart containing the "precious ointment" of love, and of sorrow, not only for your own sins, but for the sins of many in the world who do *not* show "great love." Pray for sinners at every Communion you make, and ask our Blessed Lady—the only one of us who never sinned—to pray for sinners. "Pray for us sinners now and at the hour of our death. Amen."

6. "Blessed Are the Meek"[15]

Boys—and very likely girls too sometimes—rather stupidly, think that to be meek means to be weak. It does not; it means to be strong. To be self-controlled —to be gentle, to be meek —needs strength. The only thing that our Lord definitely told us to learn of Him was just that—meekness: ". . . and learn from me, for I am meek and humble of heart."[16]

Few of us are naturally meek, but we may become so by desire, by making efforts, by prayer, and above

---

[15] St. Matthew 5:5
[16] St. Matthew 11:29

all, by contact with our Lord in Holy Communion.

Today ask Him first to help you to understand what meekness really means, and then to make you meek in the true sense of the word.

Then turn to our Lady and say:
> *Virgo singularis*
> *Inter omnes mitis*
> *Nos culpis solutes*
> *Mites fac et castos.*

(Maiden, gentler and more pure than all others, make us, delivered from sin, meek and stainless.)

7. THE SOLDIER WHO ASKED OUR LORD TO CURE HIS SERVANT

Read about him in St. Matthew 8:5-13, or in St. Luke 7:1-10, and pray to think about others and to ask for things of God for *them,* not always for yourselves. Pray also for strong faith in God's power, like the centurion's.

Meditation

I Talk with God in Meditation

Outlines to Be Filled In

There are lots of subjects which lend themselves to being divided into seven parts, and which therefore would give you opportunities of making for yourselves little meditations and prayers for many a week of Communions.

The Seven Parts of the Our Father
1. Our Father, Who art in heaven, hallowed be Thy name
2. Thy Kingdom come
3. Thy will be done on earth as it is in heaven
4. Give us this day our daily bread
5. Forgive us our trespasses as we forgive those who trespass against us
6. Lead us not into temptation
7. Deliver us from evil

Look up answers 147 to 157 in *The Penny Catechism*, which will give you ideas for prayers about these seven divisions of the Our Father.

The Seven Parts of the Hail Mary
1. Hail Mary, full of grace
2. The Lord is with thee
3. Blessed art thou amongst women
4. Blessed is the fruit of thy womb, Jesus
5. Holy Mary, Mother of God
6. Pray for us sinners, now
7. And at the hour of our death

These will serve for seven little prayers that you can make yourself—one to say each day with your other prayers at Communion—prayers something like this: "Mary, you never sinned; you are *full* of grace and quite pleasing to God, and so we may feel proud of you, and be glad that God chose you for His mother. Pray for me and get me more grace, especially . . ."

If you think about the different parts of the Hail Mary, and make short prayers on each part like this, the words will come to mean much more to you. The Hail Mary will have become a little meditation.

THE SEVEN LAST JOURNEYS OF OUR LORD
1. From the cenacle, the room where He had celebrated the Last Supper, to the Garden of Gethsemane[17]
2. From the Garden of Gethsemane, where He was taken prisoner, to the house of Annas, the ex-High Priest[18]
3. From the house of Annas to that of Caiphas, the High Priest[19]
4. From the house of Caiphas to the other side of Jerusalem to be brought before Pilate, the Roman Governor[20]
5. From Pilate to Herod[21]
6. From Herod back to Pilate[22]
7. From Pilate to Calvary[23]

---
[17] St. Matthew 26:30
[18] St. John 18:13
[19] St. John 18:24
[20] St. Matthew 27:2
[21] St. Luke 23:6-7
[22] St. Luke 23:11
[23] St. Mark 15:22

Meditation

These would be suitable subjects to think about and pray about at Holy Communion during Lent, and especially in Passion Week or Holy Week. You might sometimes take one of them for a Communion made on any Friday.

If you find it difficult to make a prayer about *each* journey, perhaps you could make one about all the seven together.

Our Lord had no rest, nor food, nor sleep during these long and painful hours from the time He left the Upper Room on Holy Thursday evening until three o' clock of the afternoon of Good Friday, when He died on the Cross.

Pray to realize now, while you are young, the evil of sin which caused all this suffering and much more.

Ask for true sorrow for your sins and for the spirit which will make you ready to do penance for them.

OUR LORD'S SEVEN LAST WORDS

1. "Father, forgive them, they know not what they do."[24]
2. "Amen, I say to you, today you will be with me in Paradise."[25]
3. "Woman, behold, your son . . . Behold, your mother."[26]
4. "My God, my God, why have you forsaken me?"[27]
5. "I thirst."[28]

---

[24] St. Luke 23:34
[25] St. Luke 23:43
[26] St. John 19:26-27
[27] St. Matthew 27:46
[28] St. John 19:28

6. "It is finished."[29]
7. "Father, into your hands I commend my spirit."[30]

These also might serve as subjects of thought and prayer for a week of Communions during Lent or Passiontide. If each word is well thought over, it will not be difficult to frame prayers about them:

Jesus, You prayed for Your enemies, for Your very executioners, and even when dying in agony excused them and asked God's forgiveness for them.

In this Communion give me something of that wonderful spirit of mercy and forgiveness.

Mary, who, standing at the foot of the Cross, heard those words, ask your Son to make me compassionate and generous in forgiving those who annoy or offend or do me harm.

St. John, you, we know, only became gentle and forgiving by degrees, and you had just the same help as I have—Holy Communion. Obtain for me from the Master you loved so well something of your personal love of Him and of your readiness to love and forgive others for His sake.

THE SEVEN GIFTS OF THE HOLY SPIRIT

Please think about these gifts and make a prayer about each of them for Communion time.

1. Wisdom – The gift of wisdom teaches us a sense of values. By it, we come to realize that the things that last forever are the things that matter.

---

[29] St. John 19:30
[30] St. Luke 23:46

Meditation

2. Understanding – This gift is like a light suddenly turned on that makes things we could not see before quite plain and clear. Through this gift of the Holy Spirit, we come to realize and appreciate the truths of our faith.
3. Counsel – Helps us not to be impetuous and do things we are sorry for directly afterwards, but to go to a wise friend for advice, and above all to ask *God's* advice before we take any important step.
4. Fortitude – Means bravery in our religious life, courage to fight against temptation, and—even if we get the worst of it, and *do* fall into sin—to get up and go on fighting again. There will be hard things in our life, probably, that we simply could not face without this gift, but it was given to us in the Sacrament of Confirmation, and helps us when the need for it comes.
5. Knowledge – This gift is rather like that of wisdom; it seems to follow after it, as the thread does the needle. Wisdom makes us wise in the things of God and makes us take *His* view of the things of this world. Knowledge makes us wise in our use of earthly things and teaches us that they too, as well as what is more directly spiritual, can be *made* pleasing to God. Pray hard at Holy Communion for this gift, because we spend so much time in doing things which *in themselves* are of no value, that we want to increase our knowledge of how to *make* them of value. Giving our day to God by means of the Morning Offering is one good way.
6. Piety – "Pious," like "meek," is a word boys often misunderstand. It does not mean "goody-goody,"

any more than meek means "weak." The Holy Spirit's gift of piety makes the service of God agreeable and not difficult. It makes prayer less of a task and more of a pleasure. Our Lord spoke of His "burden" as being "light." The gift of piety helps to make it so. When we carry a load to please someone, it seems less heavy than it really is. It is like that with piety. It is given to us to make our service of God a loving and willing service.[31]

7. Fear of the Lord – If we know that God is good and merciful, and if we therefore love Him, why should we fear Him? He Himself said to His Apostles that they were to fear His judgments, His punishments —therefore the gift of fear of the Lord makes us fear *sin,* for which God must punish, and fear it for a higher reason, too, because it displeases God. It is better to serve God from love, but fear is a good foundation for love. St. Ignatius prayed that if ever the love of God should die down in his heart then at least might the fear of hell keep him from sinning. If a saint prayed like that, we may well do so too.

---

[31] One has heard boys say that pious people put them off. These people's piety cannot be genuine. Pray for an increase of the *real* piety that does not *hinder,* but helps, others.

Meditation

I Talk with God through the Prayer of St. Thomas Aquinas

Adoro Te devote latens Deitas

1.
Adoro Te devote latens Deitas,
Quae sub his figuris vere latitas:
Tibi se cor meum totum subjicit,
Quia Te contemplans totum deficit.

Devoutly I adore You, hidden God. Hidden, but truly *here,* in Your disguise of bread and wine. I cannot *see* You, but I *believe* You are here before me.

2.
Visus, tactus, gustus in Te fallitur,
Sed auditu solo tuto creditur:
Credo quidquid dixit Dei Filius,
Nil hoc verbo Veritatis verius.

Sight, touch and taste are all at fault, but I can trust my *hearing.* I believe what you have *said.* There is no truer word than the *Word*—Truth Itself.

3.
In cruce latebat sola Deitas,
At hie latet simul et humanitas;
Ambo tamen credens, atque confitens
Peto quod petivit latro poenitens.

As *God,* You were hidden on the Cross, but in the Host as Man too You are hidden. I believe and confess that both as God and as Man You are really here, and to You I make the same prayer as the good thief, "Remember me in Your Kingdom."

4.
Plagas, sicut Thomas non intueor,
Deum tamen meum Te confiteor,
Fac me tibi semper magis credere,
In Te spem habere, Te diligere.

I do not see Your wounds as Thomas saw them, but I too confess You to be my Lord and my God. Make me ever *believe* in You more, *hope* in You more, *love* You more.[32]

5.
O memoriale mortis Domini,
Panis vivus, vitam praestans homini:
Praesta meae menti de Te vivere
Et Te illi semper dulce sapere.

O Remembrance of Jesus' death, Living Bread bestowing life on men, be ever Life to *my* soul! Let me know something of Your sweetness.

6.
Pie Pelicane, Jesu Domine,
Me immundum munda tuo sanguine:

---

[32] "Increase my *faith.*" "Fix all my *hope* in You." "Bind my heart to Yours in deathless *love.*" (Learn by heart these short Acts of Faith, Hope, and Love and say them often.)

Meditation

Cujus una stilla salvum facere
Totum mundum quit ab omni scelere.

Loving Pelican, Jesus, Lord, I am unclean; please cleanse me in Your Blood. One drop would be enough to make a whole world pure.

7.
Jesu quern velatum nunc aspicio
Oro fiat illud, quod tarn sitio,
Ut Te revelata cernens facie,
Visu sim beatus Tuae gloriae.   Amen.

Jesus *now* I only see you veiled, but I look forward so much to the day when I shall clearly see Your face, when I shall gaze on You in all Your Glory.

Amen.

Prayer and Meditation

by Janet P. McKenzie, OCDS

Prayer and Meditation

Prayer—talking with and listening to God—and meditation—prayerful reflection or holy thinking—are ways to discover the mystery of God, ways to get to know Him better. No one can teach you to pray, except God. But in order to help God reveal Himself to you, begin by focusing on the following:

1. Find a Holy Place

To really concentrate on God, to focus all your attention on Him without distraction, it is important to find a place where you feel close to Him. Perhaps you can create a prayer corner in your house (or in your bedroom). If possible, go to church to pray in front of the Blessed Sacrament. You may want to find a special place outside where you can pray. Find a place where you can be alone with God. Although it is not necessary to be alone when you pray, it is very helpful at first to look for God within by surrounding yourself with only those things that remind you of Him.

2. Keep a Holy Quiet

God reveals Himself to you in silence. You cannot hear His voice or feel His presence when you are surrounded by noise. Just as Jesus did many times in the Bible, you need to get away from the noise and activities of your life. In silence, you are able to talk with and listen to God. To allow God to teach you to pray, it is helpful to be alone and very quiet. Prayer and meditation are learned easier in the school of silence.

Teach yourself to keep your mind and heart clear and quiet so you may better think about and listen to God.

3. Stay in Holy Stillness

Sit or kneel in a comfortable position, paying close attention to your own stillness. Try not to move your arms, your hands, your legs, your feet. Your body is still—even your breathing is quiet. But the silence and stillness needed to find God is not an empty silence. Close your eyes and listen to the little sounds around you. This relaxed stillness will help you listen to what God wants to tell you and help you to respond to Him. Teach yourself to quiet your body and be totally still.

4. Talk with Loving Words

You can talk with God by using prayers written by others, prayers you have memorized, prayers you make up yourself. God loves to simply hear about your day, your worries, the things you are thankful for, your hurts, and your victories. You may say short prayers to Him, over and over—"Amen," "I love You," "Alleluia," "Thank you." You can slowly recite and think about short passages from the psalms: "The Lord is king; let the earth rejoice" (Psalm 97:1), "The Lord is my light and my salvation" (Psalm 27:1), or "The Lord is my shepherd; I shall not want" (Psalm 23:1). You can read prayers from a prayer card. You may want to look at a holy picture and talk to God about what you see. Look at a crucifix and quietly think about how Jesus suffered for you. Awakening your love for God makes it easier to pray.

Prayer and Meditation

You may talk with God about someone you know or about yourself. You may sit in silence and admire the sunset, a flower, a tree, a rainbow, a cloud. You cannot see God (Can you see Love?) but you can talk with Him whenever you want. He is always there; He is always listening. Teach yourself not to say much when you pray but to love much.

5. LISTEN TO GOD

Prayer is more than talking with God. In a real conversation, both people speak. An old Arab proverb tells us that God gave us two ears and one month so that we can listen twice as much as we talk. Listening to God is as important as talking with Him. Teach yourself to wait in silence to hear Him speak.

St. Joan of Arc often talked about the voices she heard when she prayed. Some people asked her why she thought she was so special that the saints and angels would speak to her when they don't speak to other people. She is said to have told them that they *do* speak to other people—but most people don't listen. Teach yourself to listen to God speaking in your soul.

Sometimes when God speaks, you may not know it is Him. He may not speak out loud like people do. He may speak by putting good thoughts or ideas into your head—sometimes thoughts not really related to what you were thinking or praying about at the time. Sometimes it is a voice inside you that seems to speak—a voice some people call their conscience, a voice that tells you not to do something or calls you to be a better person. Teach yourself to recognize the voice of God.

Sometimes when God speaks, you may not like what He says. He may answer your prayer by saying "No." He loves You and wants you to have everything You need to be happy. But He also knows better than you what will truly make you happy. Know that God hears all your prayers and wants only what is best for you. Teach yourself to accept His answers to your prayers even when His answer is not what you wanted.

That is not to say that God will speak to you every time you pray. But even if He seems silent, He is still there, just as the sun is on a cloudy day. Teach yourself to love God even when He is silent.

Sometimes too God's answers to your prayers are not immediate. God often speaks to us through other people. Someone may say something to you that is an answer to your prayer to God. Something may happen in your life that you can easily see as a loving action of God. Sometimes too you may—through your words or actions—be an answer to someone else's prayer. Teach yourself to see God's presence—His love—in the people and events of your life. Help others to see God's love and action through you.

With practice, you will become better at loving God by thinking holy thoughts. You will become better at listening for Him and recognizing His voice in your heart and in the voices of other people. As you become better friends with Him, you will see His loving hand in all the events of your life. Teach yourself to watch for all the little loving surprises He places in your life each day. Watch for His love—it's always there!

Read-aloud Children's Books on Prayer and Meditation

1. *The Ball of Red String* by Sister Marlene Halpin, published by Loyola Press – A guided meditation that takes children to a quiet place where they can meet Jesus. This booklet teaches us all that we can talk to Jesus anytime, anywhere, and about anything.

2. *In My Heart Room: 21 Love Prayers for Children* by Sister Mary Terese Donze, published by Ligouri Publications – Teaches meditation to children by helping them focus on common objects such as a coin, flower, pencil etc. This book, which combines Volumes 1-3 of the now out-of-print original series, encourages children to enter into their heart room where they experience Jesus living within them.

3. *The King of the Golden City Study Edition* by Mother Mary Loyola, published by Biblio Resource Publications – Illustrates the progression of a little girl's prayer life and Jesus' desire to share an intimate relationship with each one of His children. Unique to the study edition is the section that explores, for older children and adults, the art of prayer in the spirit of the three Carmelite Doctors of the Catholic Church.

4. *The Monk Who Grew Prayer* by Claire Brandenburg, published Conciliar Press – A child's picture book that, like the selections above, also has much to teach adults about prayer. As the monk prays through his daily tasks, we learn how to pray no matter where we are or what we are doing.

Adult Resources on Children's Prayer

1. *Listening to God with Children, The Montessori Method Applied to the Catechesis of Children* by Gianna Gobbi (Translated and edited by Rebekah Rojoewicz), published by Treehaus Communications – Written for parents and teachers to invite them to "enter into the secret of childhood" and to "journey with the child toward God." This resource is helpful in understanding the spiritual experiences of young children and in leading them toward deeper prayer.

2. *Children Praying: Why and How to Pray with Your Children* by Joan Bel Geddes, published by Sorin Books, an imprint of Ave Maria Press – Now out of print, but a good general manual for sharing prayer with children. Full of insightful quotations, this book is helpful to families who wish to explore prayer together.

More RACE for Heaven Products

RACE for Heaven study guides use the saint biographies of Mary Fabyan Windeatt to teach the Catholic faith to all members of your family. Written with your family's various learning levels in mind, these flexible study guides succeed as stand-alone unit studies or supplements to your regular curriculum. Thirty to sixty minutes per day will allow your family to experience:

- ☑ The spirituality and holy habits of the saints
- ☑ Lively family discussions on important faith topics
- ☑ Increased critical thinking and reading comprehension skills
- ☑ Quality read-aloud time with Catholic "living books"
- ☑ Enhanced knowledge of Catholic doctrine and the Bible
- ☑ History and geography incorporated into saintly literature
- ☑ Writing projects based on secular and Catholic historical events and characters

Purchase these guides individually or in the following grade-level packages. (Grades are determined solely on the length of each book in the series.)

Grades 3-4: *St. Thomas Aquinas, The Story of the "Dumb Ox"*; *St. Catherine of Siena, The Girl Who Saw Saints in the Sky*; *Patron Saint of First Communicants, The Story of Blessed Imelda Lambertini*; and *The Miraculous Medal, The Story of Our Lady's Appearances to St. Catherine Labouré*

Grade 5: *St. Rose, First Canonized Saint of the Americas*; *St. Martin de Porres, The Story of the Little Doctor of Lima, Peru*; *King David and His Songs, A Story of the Psalms*; and *Blessed Marie of New France, The Story of the First Missionary Sisters in Canada*

Grade 6: *St. Dominic, Preacher of the Rosary and Founder of the Dominicans; St. Benedict, The Story of the Father of the Western Monks; The Children of Fatima and Our Lady's Message to the World;* and *St. John Masias, Marvelous Dominican Gate-keeper of Lima, Peru*

Grade 7: *The Little Flower, The Story of St. Therese of the Child Jesus; St. Hyacinth, The Story of the Apostle of the North; The Curé of Ars, The Story of St. John Vianney, Patron Saint of Parish Priests;* and *St. Louis de Montfort, The Story of Our Lady's Slave*

Grade 8: *Pauline Jaricot, Foundress of the Living Rosary and the Society for the Propagation of Faith; St. Francis Solano, Wonder-Worker of the New World and Apostle of Argentina and Peru; St. Paul the Apostle, The Story of the Apostle to the Gentiles;* and *St. Margaret Mary, Apostle of the Sacred Heart*

The Windeatt Dictionary: Pre-Vatican II Terms and Catholic Words from Mary Fabyan Windeatt's Saint Biographies explains over 450 Catholic terms and expressions used in this popular saint biography series. Indispensable in expanding knowledge and practice of the Catholic faith, this book provides a ready access for the Catholic vocabulary words used in the RACE for Heaven Windeatt study guides. This dictionary also includes a Catholic book report resource that contains suggestions for forty-five Catholic book reports: fourteen writing projects, ten book report activities, and twenty-one topics for saint biographies.

Graced Encounters with Mary Fabyan Windeatt's Saints: 344 Ways to Imitate the Holy Habits of the Saints is a compilation of the "Growing in Holiness" sections of RACE for Heaven's Catholic study guides for the Windeatt saint biography series and presents 344 examples of saintly behavior, one for nearly every chapter in each of these twenty biographies. Enhance your encounter with the saints by practicing the models of devotion, service, penance, prayer, and virtue offered in this guide.

Bedtime Bible Stories for Catholic Children: Loving Jesus through His Word contains twenty discussions of Bible stories that were originally published in serial form in a Catholic children's magazine. Their author stated, "The tales are extremely simple and unadorned. They are real conversations of a real child and her mother." Due to popular demand, the series was later (1910) published as a book, *Bible Stories Told to "Toddles."* The engaging conversational style of this book lends itself well as a bedtime read-aloud that allows Jesus to come alive in the Gospels. The study aids include discussion questions to help foster spiritual conversation, Bible excerpts relevant to the presented story, "Growing in Holiness" suggestions for living the Gospel message in our daily lives, and short catechism lessons for both children and adults.

Communion with the Saints: A Family Preparation Program for First Communion and Beyond in the Spirit of St. Therese imitates St. Therese of the Child Jesus and her family who studied and prayed for sixty-nine days in anticipation of Therese's First Holy Communion. Modeling this preparation, the *Communion with the Saints* program will help any family find renewed fervor in the reception of the Eucharist. This resource includes a chapter-by-chapter study of the following four books:

- *The Little Flower, The Story of Saint Therese of the Child Jesus*—to provide the foundation of God's love for us and to encourage a desire for holiness

- *The Children of Fatima and Our Lady's Message to the World*—to show the sinfulness of our world and the need to avoid sin

- *The Patron Saint of First Communicants, The Story of Blessed Imelda Lambertini*—to inspire devotion to the Sacrament of Holy Communion

- *The King of the Golden City* by Mother Mary Loyola—to illustrate Jesus' Presence as a source of grace necessary to live a holy life

Each of the sixty-nine days of preparation includes read-aloud selections with enrichment activities, meditational readings, catechism lessons, and plenty of practical application to promote a growth in holiness and sanctity. Weekend suggestions include a list of over thirty-five family projects. The use of *My First Communion Journal* is encouraged with this program.

My First Communion Journal in Imitation of Saint Therese of the Child Jesus provides a lasting keepsake of a child's First Holy Communion. Saint Therese of the Child Jesus and her family studied and prayed for sixty-nine days prior to Therese's First Holy Communion. This journal imitates that family model of preparation for the reception of the Most Holy Eucharist. Each daily entry contains a stanza of a poem composed by Saint Therese, a quotation from Saint Faustina Kowalska's diary (*Divine Mercy in My Soul*), or a Scripture quotation. Two weekly themes—a floral theme in imitation of Saint Therese and a battle theme molded from the teachings of Saint Paul—are offered with accompanying weekly passages from Scripture suitable for memorization. This journal may be completed in conjunction with the *Communion with the Saints* program or used separately.

More RACE for Heaven Products

The King of the Golden City Study Edition is a new edition of a book that was originally published in 1921. This treasure of a book was written in response to a student's appeal for instructions along with "little stories" to help her prepare for Holy Communion. To fulfill this request, Mother Loyola of the Bar Convent in York, England, wrote a simple story that illustrates Jesus' desire to share an intimate relationship with each one of His children. This new edition contains some updated language but, quite deliberately, does not contain any pictures. Readers, as they progress through this story, will form a mental image of their King, one as unique and personal as their own relationship with Him. The study sections assist with the allegory, connect to the Bible as well as to the catechism, and explore the art of prayer in the spirit of the three Carmelite Doctors of the Church. Although written over eighty-five years ago for a young child, this book remains a timeless masterpiece of Catholic literature suitable for all ages. (Also available as a study guide only)

The Good Shepherd and His Little Lambs Study Edition is a simply told Catholic tale of four children who meet with their beloved aunt for "First Communion talks." More than a story, it is a First Communion primer that takes the tenets of the catechism and, through naturally-flowing conversations, relates them in the language of little ones to authentic Christian living. As Mrs. Bosch explains, "We might learn the catechism all the way through beautifully, and at the end find ourselves still very stiff and clumsy about loving our Lord. When He comes to us, we don't want to welcome Him into our souls only with answers out of the catechism, do we?" Enriched by appropriate Biblical passages, points of doctrine, and prayers, this story-primer is an enjoyable and effective read-aloud that will prepare the Good Shepherd's little lambs to worthily receive Him in the Holy Eucharist.

A Reconciliation Reader-Retreat: Read-Aloud Lessons, Stories, and Poems for Young Catholics Preparing for Confession provides a basic doctrinal explanation and review of the Sacrament of Reconciliation as well as a Gospel examination of conscience—a seven-day read-aloud formation retreat. To help the lessons come alive and to enable young Catholics to more readily apply these doctrines to their own daily lives, the lessons have been supplemented with pertinent short stories and poems. Each lesson contains reflection questions, a family prayer, and a "Gospel Examination of Conscience" that is formulated according to the dictates of the *Catechism of the Catholic Church*. This reader-retreat will not only enrich and deepen the sacramental experience for each member of your family but it will also provide several tools to help you recommit to leading a virtuous life and to grow together in holiness.

Alternative Book Reports for Catholic Students contains forty-five book report ideas to encourage critical thinking for ages seven to fourteen. These ideas are intended to provoke a reflection on those themes and topics that support and encourage Catholic living as well as some that may conflict with our Faith. Many report topics require an examination of our personal faith life and prompt us to take lessons from the saints to strengthen our own faith in God. The suggested activities vary from written exercises to creative art projects and include twenty-one topics specifically designed for saint biographies. Other activities can be used within a group or family.

Reading the Saints: Lists of Catholic Books for Children Plus Book Collecting Tips for the Home and School Library (formerly entitled *Saintly Resources*) is a valuable tool for Catholic home educators, classroom teachers, and collectors of Catholic juvenile books. *Reading the Saints* will help you discover living books from such popular out-of-print Catholic juvenile series as Catholic Treasury, Vision Books, and American Background Books as well as current series books for young Catholics. Use this book to find:

- Over 800 Catholic books listed by author, series, reading level, century, and geographical location
- More than 275 authors of saint biographies, historical fiction, and poetry written for Catholic juvenile readers
- Publishers of Catholic children's books, present and past
- Helpful advice for collecting and caring for used books
- Hundreds of age-appropriate, accessible living books to enrich your study of the Catholic Church's rich heritage of saints and notable Catholic historical figures
- Information on how to build and maintain your own library of Catholic juvenile books
- Inspiring quotations about book collecting, reading, and the love of books

The Outlaws of Ravenhurst Study Edition contains a classic story of the persecution of Scottish Catholics that was first written in 1923 and was revised and reprinted in 1950. This 2009 edition of Sr. M. Imelda Wallace's *Outlaws of Ravenhurst* contains the revised story of 1950 plus chapter-by-chapter aids to assist readers in assimilating the book's strong Catholic elements into their wn lives. The study section focuses on critical thinking, integration of biblical teachings, and the study of the virtuous life to which Christ calls us as mature Catholics. With its emphasis on virtues (theological and moral plus the gifts and fruits of the Holy Spirit), the spiritual and corporal works of mercy, and the Beatitudes, *Outlaws of Ravenhurst Study Edition* is a fun and effective catechetical tool for Catholics preparing for the Sacrament of Confirmation. (Also available as a study guide only)

The Family that Overtook Christ Study Edition: The Story of the Family of St. Bernard of Clairvaux is an excellent read for young adults who are preparing to receive the Sacrament of Confirmation. In this exciting chronicle of the life of twelfth-century knights, we have an entire family of nine saints who lay before us their individual means of achieving intimate union with Christ. Learn with the Fontaines family how to supernaturalize the natural, develop a God-consciousness, and attain sanctity by being yourself. Perfect for high-school read-aloud (or adult study), this new study edition has over 250 footnotes for increased comprehension and provides discussion/meditation points to promote the art of spiritual conversation. The appendix lists formulas of Catholic doctrine that are essential for confirmands not only to know but also to incorporate into their own spiritual lives.

A Confirmation Reader-Retreat: Read-Aloud Lessons, Stories and Poems for Young Catholics utilizes chapters from two excellent out-of-print Catholic books for children (*I Belong to God, Great Truths in Simple Stories for Children and Lovers of Children* by Lillian Clark; and *Children's Retreats in Preparation for First Confession, First Holy Communion, and Confirmation* by Rev. P.A. Halpin). This book provides a basic doctrinal review of the Sacrament of Confirmation as well as prayer experiences—a nine-day read-aloud retreat/novena. The reprinted material has been supplemented with short stories and poems

More RACE for Heaven Products

that provide insights in applying catechetical doctrines to the daily life of young Catholics. Each lesson concludes with "I Talk with God"—a section that encourages readers (of all ages) to deepen their relationship with each of the Three Persons of the Blessed Trinity. Reflection questions promote the habit of spiritual conversation within your family—to encourage family members to discuss holy topics—and to help you grow together in holiness. Additionally, a traditional novena to the Holy Spirit is included.

To Order: Email info@RACEforHeaven.com or place an order from RACEforHeaven.com. Discover, MasterCard, VISA, PayPal, American Express, checks, and money orders are accepted.

CPSIA information can be obtained
at www.ICGtesting.com
Printed in the USA
LVHW11s0415181018
594006LV00001B/120/P